WALKING A
TIGHTROPE

Women and Veiling in the United Kingdom

Ayesha Salma Kariapper

محوانٹیں ذیر اثر مُسلم قوانیں
Women Living Under Muslim Laws
النساء في ظل قوانين المسلمين
Femmes sous lois musulmanes

International Solidarity Network

Walking a Tightrope
Women and Veiling in the United Kingdom
Ayesha Salma Kariapper

First Edition
Copyright © Women Living Under Muslim Laws, 2009

Published by:
Women Living Under Muslim Laws
PO BOX 28445
London
N19 5NZ, UK

Email: wluml@wluml.org
Website: www.wluml.org

Printed and bound by:
The Russell Press, Nottingham, UK

Cover design by:
Kika Miller

Design and typography by:
Tristram Ariss, design@arissdesign.com

ISBN-13: 978-0-9544943-8-4

To my husband, Ahmed:

"Zubaan tak jo na aa'aye
woh muhabbat aur hoti hai
fasana aur hota hai
haqiqat aur hoti hai"

To Ammi:

for showing me what a strong woman is.

To Bhaia:

for always pushing me to be better than the best I can be.

Walking a Tightrope: Women and Veiling in the United Kingdom is a publication of the International Solidarity Network, Women Living Under Muslim Laws. WLUML publications aim at providing information about lives, struggles and strategies of women living in diverse Muslim communities and countries.

The information contained in WLUML publications does not necessarily represent the views and positions of the compilers or of the network Women Living Under Muslim Laws, unless stated.

WLUML publications are meant to make accessible to a wide readership the broadest possible strands of opinion within varied movements or initiatives promoting greater autonomy of women living in Muslim contexts. The publications seek to inform and help share different experiences, strategies and interpretations.

Contents

Page

vii **Acknowledgements**

ix **Glossary**

1 **Chapter 1: Introduction**

9 **Chapter 2: Methodology**

15 **Chapter 3: A Profile of the Muslim Population of Britain**

19 **Chapter 4: Identity Assertion or Divide and Rule?**
19 4.1 Evolution of Muslim Community Activism
27 4.2 British Muslim Women in Community Activism
34 4.3 Proliferation of Dress codes Ideology
39 4.4 Women's Experiences of Veiling

45 **Chapter 5: Faith-Based Schools**

55 **Chapter 6: Veiling and Empowerment Strategies**
55 6.1 Demanding space for Veiling in British Schools
67 6.2 Discrimination in the Labour Market
74 6.3 Competing for Sports Facilities

83 **Chapter 7: The View from Europe**
83 7.1 Republic of Ireland
86 7.2 France
89 7.3 Germany
94 7.4 Sweden
97 7.5 Turkey

101 **Chapter 8: Conclusion**

105 **Endnotes**

111 **Bibliography**

118 **About the Author**

119 **Index**

Acknowledgements

I am grateful to Professor Homa Hoodfar (Concordia University, Montreal) and Farida Shaheed (Shirkat Gah – Women's Resource Centre, Lahore) for selecting me to undertake this research for the International Feminist Solidarity Network, Women Living Under Muslim Laws (WLUML). I also thank Professor Hoodfar and Anissa Hélie (John Jay College, New York), whose guidance, editing and review helped refined this final manuscript.

The research was initiated as part of the dress code discourse and sexuality research program of the Women Living Under Muslim Laws network. It was conceptualised as part of the WLUML component of the Women's Empowerment in Muslim Contexts (WEMC) research that provided conceptual guidance and support and invited me to conduct the research.

I would also like to acknowledge the Network for Social Change Ltd., for recognising the significance of this research and providing funding to WLUML for the project, and NORAD for funding the design and printing of this book.

I would like to thank Chiara Maurilio, Publications Officer at WLUML for her essential role in coordinating the publication and dissemination of this book.

Special thanks are due to my dear friends, Saman Jamal, for helping to conceptualise the cover design and Eleanor Kilroy for her meticulous copy-editing of the text.

This acknowledgment would be incomplete without mentioning the moral support of my mother, Rehana M. Kariapper and my brother, Amanullah Jiffrey Kariapper.

Last, but not the least, this work would not have been possible without the love, patience, support and constant encouragement of my husband, Muhammad Ahmed Shamim. In short, I would like to thank him for everything he has had to put up with while I was writing this book.

Ayesha Salma Kariapper
London, 9 November 2009

Glossary

Burqa: Also spelled *burka*, this is an outer garment worn in various styles in South Asia including Afghanistan for the purpose of veiling. It is a loose cloak which usually covers the body from head to toe. The Afghan design (typically blue in colour) has a patch of net sewn into it so that the wearer can see, but her eyes are not visible. This style is also worn in the North West Frontier Province and Balochistan province of Pakistan. In the rest of Pakistan, the *burqa* (traditionally black) usually consists of a loose, full-sleeved, full-length cloak with buttons in front and a separate scarf to wrap around the head. The scarf has an optional transparent cloth attached which can be pulled down to veil the face.

Chador: In Iran, this is a long semicircle of fabric, which is wrapped to cover the whole female body from head to toe except the face. It is usually black and worn as an outer garment by women. In Pakistan, it is spelled *chadder*, it is available in all colours and it is made of a long rectangular cloth, which can be of any material, such as wool in winter, cotton or other fabrics in summer. Traditionally, it is worn loosely wrapped around the upper part of the body and over the head. The length and width of the cloths, and therefore the extent to which it covers the woman's body, varies from community to community.

Dars: or *dars-e-Qur'an* refers to the structured lessons and courses conducted by an Islamic scholar for groups of men or women to explain the full historical context and translation, and to discuss the full meaning and interpretation of each verse of the Qur'an. Typically, the Qur'an is read and discussed chapter by chapter and these lessons last 6 months to a year.

Dupatta: This is a long scarf (typically measuring two-and-a-half yards), which is draped around the head or neck and chest, and worn with the *shalwar kameez*. The *dupatta* is matched with the fabric, pattern and style of the *shalwar kameez*. For the many who do not wear it as an alternative to the *chador* or *chadder*, it is a stylish accessory worn over one shoulder or across the chest and over both shoulders.

Hadith: This is a term used for the reported sayings of the Prophet Muhammad (PBUH). *Ahadith* is the plural form.

Hajj: This is an Arabic word which refers to the Muslims' pilgrimage to Mecca (Saudi Arabia). It is the fifth pillar (of faith) in Islam and represents an obligation which must be carried out by all Muslims at least once in their lifetime provided that they have the capacity (in terms of health as well as financial resources) to undertake the journey. It is currently the largest annual pilgrimage in the world which attracts millions of Muslims from many different countries. The *hajj* occurs once a year from the 8 to the 13 day of the twelfth month of the Islamic (lunar) calendar.

Halal: It literally means 'lawful' in Arabic. It is usually used to refer to food whose consumption is permissible according to the *Shari'a* and it is opposite to the word *haram* (see definition below).

Haram: It literally means 'forbidden', 'prohibited', and 'sacred'. This term can refer to things, persons and behaviours.

Hijab: It comes from the Arab verb *hajaba* that means 'to veil, hide, conceal'. Probably the most common style of veiling in the Muslim diasporas in the west, the *hijab* is a simple square piece of cloth folded into a triangle and wrapped around the head. It is fastened under the chin or the sides such that the face is visible but the neck and hair are covered. Today, the *hijab* is available in many different fabrics, styles and colours.

Jilbab: The *jilbab* is an outer garment worn for the purpose of veiling by women. It is a long cloak which covers the entire body except the hands, feet, face and head. Typically, the *jilbab* is worn with either a *hijab* or *niqab* covering the head. It is commonly worn in some Middle Eastern countries in the Gulf region, such as Saudi Arabia and the United Arab Emirates, and has been adopted among sections of the British Muslim community as well.

Kalimah: The word *kalimah* literally means 'word' in Arabic. There are six main *Kalimah* in Islam which can be explained as declarations of faith.

Khimar: This Arabic word literally means 'head covering'. The importance of this word in the debate about whether and what type of garment is perceived as modest for women in Islam is due to the fact that the plural form of this word (*khumur*) is mentioned in a verse of the Qur'an (*Surah Nur*). The translation and interpretation of this word is important in this debate. Those who do not believe that veiling is compulsory in Islam claim that the *khimar* was a piece of cloth worn by most women in Arabia at the time of the Prophet (PBUH) to help protect them from the scorching heat of the desert sun. Others use the same word in the verse to substantiate their claim that Islam does indeed require all women to wear a headscarf and/or other forms of veiling to preserve modesty.

Mahram: This is an Arabic word used to refer to members of the opposite sex (who have reached puberty) and with whom marriage and sexual intercourse is not permissible. In Islam, a woman's opposite-sex *mahrams* fall into four categories (three categories in the strict-sense definition that does not count one's spouse). (*Mahrams* for a man can be derived in a similar manner.)

1. permanent or blood *mahrams* with whom one is *mahram* by a blood relationship:
    1. father, grandfather, great-grandfather and so on;
    2. brother;
    3. son, grandson, great-grandson;
    4. uncle, great-uncle, great-great-uncle, grandparents' uncle and so on;
    5. nephew, grandnephew, great-grandnephew and so on;

2. in-law *mahrams* with whom one becomes *mahram* by marrying someone:
    1. father-in-law;
    2. son-in-law;
    3. stepfather (mother's husband) if their marriage is consummated;
    4. stepson (husband's son) if their marriage is consummated;

3. A wet nurse with whom a man can become *mahram* because of being nursed by the same woman as an infant.

Those members of the opposite sex who do not qualify in the above categories are considered as *ghayr-mahram* or non-*mahram*.

The concept of *mahram* is important in Islam as it governs the rules of interaction with the opposite sex. For example, Muslim women who practice veiling generally do not feel obligated to wear the veil in the presence of *mahrams*. Similarly, this concept also requires Muslim women to be accompanied or escorted by *mahrams* while travelling outside their city. In the case of Saudi Arabia, it is this concept of *mahram* and non-*mahram* (*ghayr-mahram*) combined with the notion of male guardianship over women which underpin the laws requiring women not to leave the house without their *mahrams*.

Niqab: Also known as the full-face veil, the *niqab* covers the neck, hair and entire face except the wearer's eyes. There are several varieties of the *niqab* which serve the same purpose. The cloth can be fastened around the forehead so that it falls to cover the entire face with only a place cut out for the eyes. Others are fastened over the *hijab* around the bridge of the nose such that some of the forehead is still visible.

Qur'an: This is the holy book of Islam. It is regarded as divine for those who believe it to consist of the exact words of God (Allah) as revealed to the Prophet Muhammad (PBUH).

Shalwar kameez: A traditional dress worn by men and women across South Asia, it is also the national dress of Pakistan. Worn in many different styles, fabrics, patterns and colours, the dress consists of a shirt or tunic known as the *kameez* and a pair of loose trousers or pyjamas which are tightened around the waist and gradually narrow towards the ankles. For women, the *shalwar kameez* is not considered complete without the *dupatta* (see above for definition).

The length of the *kameez* varies according to fashion and can be anywhere from above the knees to a few inches above the ankles. The side seams of the *kameez* are usually cut from the hips down to the remaining length of the shirt to afford the wearer ease of movement. The *kameez* can be full-sleeved, half-sleeved or sleeveless. In Britain and India, the dress is also known as the 'Punjabi suit'.

Shari'a: or **Shariyah**. A term used to refer to the body of religious 'laws' that are said to be derived from Islam; literally, it is translated as 'the path leading to the water'. Contrary to popular belief, it must be remembered that there is no one, singular, homogenous set of Muslim laws or practices. It is important to demystify the word *shari'a* and recognise the great diversity among Muslim communities and schools of thought. Commonly, sources of Islamic Laws are believed to be the Sunnah and Qur'an. However, in the early years of Islam, the word *shari'a* was not used.

Today, the four main schools of law in Sunni Islam are *Hanafi*, *Shafi'i*, *Maliki* and *Hanbali*. In Shi'a Islam, the major school of law is *Fiqh-i-Jafariya*.

These schools of jurisprudence known as *fiqh*, developed as a system in the mid-eighth century CE. Over the ages, *shari'a* evolved to the extent it became identified with divine law rather than faith or *fiqh*. As a system of laws for Muslims, it was interpreted over 100 years after the death of the Prophet Mohammad (PBUH), by jurists in different countries. Therefore, today, the set of laws known as *shari'a* vary from one Muslim country to the other as the sources of these laws are subject to interpretation.

The debate around divine injunctions and 'law' can be clarified by the following definition of *Shari'a* given by Dr. Ziba Mir-Hosseini: *"Shari'ah is the totality of God's will as revealed to the Prophet Muhammad. Fiqh is the process of human effort to identify and extract legal rules from the sacred sources of Islam: the Qur'an and the Sunnah. Thus, the Shari'ah in Muslim belief is sacred, eternal and universal, whereas fiqh, consisting of the vast literature produced by Muslim jurists, is like any other system of jurisprudence: human, mundane, not eternal, and local. "* (Source: www.musawah.org)

Sheesha: This is a single or multi-stemmed, glass water pipe for smoking, common in the Middle East, Egypt and Turkey. A similar indigenous alternative in India and Pakistan is the *hukkah*. It operates by water filtration and indirect heat and is used for smoking tobacco including tobacco infused with other flavours.

Sunnah: This word refers to the practices of the Holy Prophet Muhammad (PBUH). These have been recorded and reported over the centuries.
Surah: An Arabic word which means a chapter of the Qur'an, there are 114 *Surahs* in the Qur'an.

Tablighi Jama'at: The Tablighi Jama'at is a Sunni, self-proclaimed reformist movement which was initiated by Maulana Ilyas in 1926 in Mewat, northern India. Literally translated from Urdu as the 'assembly of preachers', the network works at the very grass-root level to preach Islam by following the example of the Prophet Muhammad (PBUH) and the Qur'an. Today, it has evolved into a transnational movement active in India, Pakistan, Bangladesh, the UK and several other countries. The founder's six principles of preaching are: i) believing in the oneness of Allah, ii) offering the five prayers daily, iii) gaining knowledge and the remembrance of Allah, iv) respecting every Muslim, v) honesty and sincerity of intention and vi) spare time for travelling for this work. The modus operandi of the preaching involves personal service and sacrifice by dispatching groups of self-funded volunteers who spare their resources and time to visit select communities for the purposes of preaching. The length of these preaching missions varies between 3 days and 40 days. Ideologically, the Tablighi Jama'at has *Deobandi* leanings. Some observers have also sought to uncover linkages between the Jama'at and *Wahhabism* promoted by Saudi Arabia, and indications of Saudi Arabian-funded groups subsidising some of the mosques built by the movement and the travel of the volunteer missionaries. It is organised as a loose network with the international headquarters, the Nizamuddin Markaz, based in Delhi, India. There is a tradition of holding annual congregations of members with the largest held in Tongi, Bangladesh. The second largest is held in Raiwind, on the outskirts of Lahore in Pakistan. In the UK, the group's activities are coordinated by the Dewsbury Markaz in West Yorkshire. It claims to be a non-political, non-violent missionary movement and refrains from making any public political statements publicly. Since 9/11, the Tablighi Jama'at has come under scrutiny by British intelligence and security forces as some suspects of the 7 July 2005 London bombing were said to have attended the Dewsbury Markaz.

Tafseer: Referring to a commentary on the Qur'an, this is a work of exegesis that attempts to interpret and explain the meaning of the Arabic verses.

Tajweed: This refers to accents upon Arabic letters which govern the correct pronunciation of the Arabic text of the Qur'an.

Ummah: This is an Arabic word which means 'community' or 'nation'. It is often used quite liberally to refer to a diaspora or community of Muslims (what many consider to be an imagined community) all over the world.

Wahhabism: This term is used to describe the puritanical, reformist movement initiated by a Saudi preacher called Sheikh Mohamed bin Abdul al-Wahab in the mid-eighteenth century in what later became known as Saudi Arabia. In an effort to eradicate what he considered to be customary practices inconsistent with Islam, he advocated a literal translation of the Qur'an and a return to the Qur'an and *Hadith* as the only authentic, fundamental texts. He preached a return to the beliefs and practices of early Islam, which he believed extended from the Prophet to three generations later. He therefore rejected all the four main schools of Islamic jurisprudence that had evolved in later centuries. Over time, there is said to have developed a symbiotic relationship between the Kingdom of Saudi Arabia (the ruling monarchy) and the *Wahhabis* who gained in influence as the other's power rose. Most Saudis today are followers of this doctrine.

However, *Wahhabism* has been the subject of intense controversy in recent years as many associate this doctrine with an extremist and often militant Islamist agenda. Its teachings and ideology are also said to compromise women's rights and freedoms. Links have been drawn between *Wahhabism* and militant Islamist outfits engaged in armed struggles in Afghanistan, Pakistan and Kashmir. It has gained influence in many parts of the world, including Muslim majority and minority contexts through well-resourced and transnational groups propagating *Wahhabism*.

Wahhabi: A follower of *Wahhabism* (defined above) is known as a *Wahhabi*. The word is also used as an adjective to describe association with *Wahhabism* (for example *Wahhabi* literature or *Wahhabi* doctrine).

7/7: It refers to the series of coordinated suicide attacks on London's public transport network on the morning of 7 July 2005. Three bombs exploded on three London Underground trains while a fourth was detonated on a bus during the morning rush hour. Fifty-six people were killed in these incidents (including the bombers) while another 700 were injured.

9/11: It refers to a series of coordinated suicide attacks against the United States on the morning of 11 September 2001. Nineteen hijackers crashed four commercial passenger airliners as follows: two into the Twin Towers of the World Trade Center in New York City, a third into the Pentagon in Arlington, Virginia, outside Washington, D.C. and a fourth into a field near Shanksville in rural Pennsylvania. These attacks resulted in the killing of nearly 3,000 people (mostly civilians), including the 19 hijackers.

Chapter 1: Introduction

The veil has become the subject of much controversy and debate over the last decade in Western Europe, and particularly after the 2003 French ban on all conspicuous symbols of religion in state schools. In October 2006, the seasoned politician and former Foreign Secretary of the United Kingdom, Jack Straw's[1] remark that he disliked the full-face veil (alternatively known as the *niqab*) sparked a huge debate at the national level with opinion divided among the British Muslim community, Muslim leaders, wider society and senior politicians of all parties.[2] In Jack Straw's camp was Tony Blair, Prime Minister from May 1997 to June 2007, and other key figures such as the Minister for Local Government and Community Cohesion[3] who believed that the face-veil[4] was a visible marker of identity as well as a symbol of women's oppression[5]. They termed it 'a physical barrier' to effective communication between Muslim women and other members of society and considered it to be a means of separating the Muslim community from mainstream 'British' culture. This debate brought to the surface underlying tensions prevalent in multicultural societies like the UK and the ways in which mainstream discourses are dominated by a combination of a lack of understanding and mistrust of the beliefs and practices of Muslims – particularly Muslim women. Today, the 'British Muslim woman' has become a focal point for the attentions of the media, government, researchers and wider British society. Under this spotlight, the Muslim woman has come to carry a disproportionate share of the burden of representation for an entire section (2.8%) of the British population. This increased visibility has put significant pressure on her image and in many ways is steering the response of the British Muslim community.

This book examines the ways in which public debates over dress codes have shaped British Muslim women's strategies in dealing with both the limitations imposed on them in the name of religion, culture, tradition and identity within the community, and with racism and exclusion from mainstream society in the United Kingdom. It seeks to investigate the existing influences and debates on women's dress codes among British Muslims with the aim of understanding the growing appeal, acceptance and adoption of 'Islamic' forms of attire among this group (from the second and third generation of Muslim immigrants). It argues that irrespective of the original motivations of those propagating specific types of dress codes, British Muslim women are using these discourses and ideologies to negotiate important life issues within what is considered the legitimate framework of religion acceptable to them and their community. In doing so, they are challenging their traditional gender role and playing an increasingly public role. They have relied on their growing political and/or religious consciousness as well as the rights they enjoy as British citizens to make these gains. However, while they have in many ways created a new identity for themselves, the impact of this identity on Muslim women and the Muslim community itself depends equally on its reception in wider society.

The response of the majority community has been to erect new barriers. British Muslim women face hostility not only in their workplace and on the street, but also in the mainstream media. Their position is not helped by high-profile comments such as that of Labour Party constitutional affairs minister, Harriet Harman[6], who argued that the veil would be an obstacle to standing for Parliament: "If you want equality, you have to be in society, not hidden away from it."

Similarly, her peer, Bill Rammell, the Minister of State for Lifelong Learning, Further and Higher Education (2005 – 2007), supported a university ban on face veils[7].

An investigation into the development of this interest in Muslim women's dress in the UK should make reference to similar debates in other Western European countries. Whereas the nuances of the debate may vary from country to country, there is a growing suspicion of Muslim communities and a corresponding loss of trust by Muslim communities in their governments. Thus, a consequence of these public and typically ill-informed debates has been to entrench the Muslim communities' use of the veil and increase society's hostility towards it. In commissioning this research that speaks directly to the British Muslim women who do veil, WLUML hoped to contribute towards bridging a social divide and providing a platform for these women to voice their perspectives and concerns to the wider British society. It is hoped that more research into women's dress will be initiated by women from Muslim communities themselves in the future. The current, highly polemical debates often confuse the issue rather than contribute to mutual understanding.

The purpose of this study was to understand the appeal of dress codes for British Muslim women, to document their experiences and analyse the implications of these dress code practices for women living in a multicultural society. In researching this dynamic and multi-layered subject, the project not only surveyed the debates surrounding Muslim women's dress but also discussed issues that are often intertwined with the veil such as racism, gender discrimination, identity politics, Muslim youth activism and government policy.

An immediate point to make about the adoption of the *hijab* and *jilbab* by British Muslims is that these items of clothing were never part of the national or traditional dress associated with the ethnic background of the majority of Muslims in the UK. Forty-three per cent of British Muslims ascribe to Pakistani origin, and nearly sixteen per cent to Bangladeshi, according to the 2001 Census by the Office of National Statistics. While there is no data available on the number of women from these backgrounds who wear the *hijab*, it is widely acknowledged as a growing trend by the community itself and media reports. That the *hijab* has become common practice over the last decade is evident from the number of veiled women seen in public spaces today – clearly unprecedented for the UK.

Indeed, all the respondents interviewed in this study had voluntarily adopted the *hijab* and in the absence of similar precedents in their families. This at once prompts the question of what motivates young people to adopt a form of dress which is alien to their ethnic origin or their parents' generation. This leads to the speculation that their motivation may not simply be a reaction to perceptions of racial and cultural discrimination and a sense of being under siege, but also an influence of the growth of Islamic revivalist movements in Britain. These latter ideologies are promoted in the UK by a growing number of trans-national politico-religious groups.

The practice of veiling may reflect the strength of organised and often well-resourced Muslim organisations (with predominantly male leadership); however, this should not simply serve as confirmation that the *hijab* or *niqab* denotes women's oppression. The dominant discourse in the west is that the veil is disempowering and at odds with the concepts of secularism and feminism. Typically, this viewpoint is passionately refuted by proponents of the veil who consider it as liberation from the pressures of conforming to contemporary standards of beauty and being victims of media-propagated fashion. (As a side note, it is worth being aware that far from being a dull piece of cloth, the veil is marketed in many different fabrics, sizes and designs for all occasions – sports to parties – and has its own fashionable accessories such as decorative pins, etc. There are many shops in London as well as websites which specialise in marketing these garments. Therefore, the notion that the *hijab* liberates women from being fashion victims is somewhat of a myth.) The proponents of veiling furthermore assert that for women who adopt the veil of their own choice, it is an exercise of free will; it allows them to secure certain individual freedoms on offer in a western society while retaining their (Muslim) community's support. However, as this book will expand on in later sections, this is not the only basis to contest the popular perceptions that regard veiling as a reinforcement of patriarchal standards and norms. This book argues for the use of alternative frameworks of power and agency to understand the lives of veiled women in Britain. Indeed, from the fieldwork carried out for this research it is clear that far from being passive recipients of dress codes propaganda (by community media or trans-national forces), British Muslim women who voluntarily veil participate in the public sphere and are very vocal about the issues to which they attach importance. The fact that they choose to do so in what they deem as Islamic (and permissible) parameters should not be mistaken for a lack of agency. Defining their own terms of engagement, whether it takes the form of talks, study circles, religious conferences, women-only support groups or fundraising activities for charitable causes can be considered a parallel form of empowerment and one which is worthy of further investigation. Conscious of the debate about the definition of empowerment, this book agrees with WEMC's[8] definition of women's empowerment as 'an increase in their capacity to make autonomous decisions to challenge or transform power relations that impede gender equality.'

At the same time, it is important to bear in mind that these developments have not occurred in isolation from the wider political context within and outside the UK. Domestic political developments, in particular Thatcherite politics and a weakening of trade unions and anti-racist organizations, two important sites for raising Muslim community concerns, left a void for an increasingly alienated Asian youth.[9] In addition, the introduction of multiculturalism at a national policy level, in part in response to, and in an attempt to accommodate, the Welsh and Scottish nationalist movements, has had significant implications for the Muslim 'community'. Prior to this period, Islam was rarely used as a basis for community organisation or negotiation with national and local authorities. It was ethnicity and race that was at the centre of mobilisation bringing all minorities (then constituting first generation migrants) under one banner for a common agenda. This changed under the policies of the Conservative Party government of Margaret Thatcher (1979-1990), which sought to weaken civil society organisations such as labour unions and anti-racist leagues by slashing their funds. On the other hand, international developments also played a contributory role; during this same period, the United States of America and its Western European allies decided to support and promote a militant Islamic ideology by equipping, training and funding *jihadi* outfits in Afghanistan to fight a proxy war against the former Soviet Union of Russia. Saudi Arabia was invited to fund and support these policies (William Maley, 1998). The Iranian revolution and the establishment of the Islamic Republic of Iran in 1979 and the subsequent Salman Rushdie affair also significantly affected the manner in which the Muslim community regrouped and organised itself in Britain. New actors and new voices emerged, many of whom use Islam and freedom of religion as their over-arching perspective and strategy, claiming to talk on behalf of one, supposedly homogenous, British Muslim community.

As such, it is imperative to understand what the veil today offers to the British Muslim women who adopt it. Towards this end, this book is divided into eight chapters. Chapter 2, 'Methodology', provides details of the research methodology designed for this project, its advantages and limitations. Chapter 3, 'A Profile of the Muslim Population of Britain', traces Muslim migration to the UK and their demographic indicators. Chapter 4 is divided into four sub-sections which trace the evolution of Muslim institutions and their impact on the Muslim dress debate and the gender ideology of the British Muslim communities. Based on field research, section 4.4 explores the motivations and experiences of women who have adopted the veil. Chapter 5, 'Faith-based Schools', canvasses the debates surrounding the role and impact of Muslim faith-based schools in promoting notions of Muslim modesty in Britain. Chapter 6 outlines the debates surrounding the veil worn by many Muslim students and teachers as illustrated by two high-profile cases. The chapter also documents the experiences of British Muslim women wearing the veil to overcome restrictions imposed on them in daily life from their community (including mobility, access to higher education, participation in the workforce, sports). Chapter 7 draws a comparative analysis with similar debates heard in other Western European countries. Chapter 8 is the Conclusion.

Writing this book has been an enriching experience for me; I found myself challenged and inspired time and again by the commitment and determination of the many highly-motivated women whom I encountered in the process. As a young, educated woman who grew up in a fairly liberal family in Pakistan, I was heavily influenced by a notion of feminism that, by and large, regarded veiling practices as a symbol of fundamentalism or at best, an assertion of patriarchy seeking to control women's bodies. Growing up in a highly class-conscious, post-colonial country and attending the private 'English-medium', all-girls Lahore Grammar School, my frame of reference from childhood as well as those of my peers was disproportionately skewed to the supposed intellectual authority of western ideals of liberalism and individualism. I grew up reading Shakespeare, playing Bach and Mozart's symphonies in piano lessons and watching Hollywood films. The school syllabi prepared us successfully for achieving the School Certificate (University of Cambridge external examination system equivalent to O' Levels). For A' Levels, I joined the co-education Lahore College of Arts and Sciences which offered a very liberal social environment. In retrospect, my friends and I grew up fairly disconnected from the reality of life for the majority of Pakistanis in terms of social norms.

At the Lahore University of Management Sciences from where I graduated with a BSc. (Honours) in Social Sciences in 2003, these ideas were only reinforced by course reading material mainly drawn from North American academic journals and books. Incidentally, it was at this same university that I became intrigued by the question of why so many of my peers (a visible minority of the student body) were veiled. Most of these girls were outgoing, typically high academic achievers and had a good number of male friends as well. But it was always a matter of great scandal and rumour if any veiled girl was seen to be dating a boy, or attending mixed dance parties off-campus. Most people in Lahore could not reconcile such uninhibited behaviour with veiling. The underlying assumption was that veiling symbolises chastity and modesty and precludes the free mixing of the sexes. At that time, I too thought that participation in mixed dance parties contradicted the point of veiling and amounted to hypocrisy. It was difficult for me then to accept that veiling and women's emancipation did not have to be mutually exclusive.

I also equated this trend with the rise of Islamic resurgence that I observed among several fellow male students (albeit, not a majority), who were swelling the ranks of the Tablighi Jama'at[10] on campus. Seemingly regular boys would suddenly come back from term breaks with a freshly grown, typically curly beard, a white or green turban wrapped around the head and their *shalwar* or trousers folded at least two inches above the ankles. They were recruited as volunteers by members of the faculty (particularly from the Computer Science department) and other student members of the Tablighi Jama'at to engage in preaching activities (initiated by a process of self-reflection) by going to villages surrounding the city for one or two-week trips. The appeal of these trips, the sense of brotherhood and solidarity, was great among many young, energetic students. However, on joining these activities their interaction with their fellow female students steadily diminished. I interpreted this as a sign that they espoused a very strict gender ideology. What I did not realise at that time was that the motivation and behaviour of the girls who observed (what was deemed an) 'Islamic' dress were very different from those of the boys.

One could hardly escape the discussion as I saw many acquaintances and relatives, including a close childhood friend adopt the headscarf. Most seemed to be influenced through their participation in informal, women-only Qur'anic interpretation and religious discussion circles initiated by the famous Al-Huda[11] group. My attitude towards this trend was also influenced by my mother, a highly-independent career woman – a medical doctor by profession – who always stressed that religion and religiosity need not be expressed outwardly and that one's faith is more a matter of internal goodness. A believer herself, she made sure that my brother and I read the Qur'an in Arabic, learnt all the six *kalimah* by heart and the usual collection of short *surahs* at a very early age (as all good, obedient Pakistani children do). She encouraged us to be good Muslims. Being a 'good Muslim' to her mainly meant being a good human being: having good intentions, being good to other people, honest and charitable. She did not like the concept of the *hijab* which was strange to her generation of urban, educated, professional Pakistani women who had grown up in much more liberal times, and before General Zia al-Huq's Islamisation programme of the 1980s. I distinctly recall her reprimanding a younger relative who had suddenly appeared at a family gathering wearing a *hijab*, "Do you really think this is going to bring you closer to God?"

So evidently, the adoption of the various forms of headscarves and *jilbabs* is not unique to Muslim-minority countries of Europe but is fast becoming a popular trend among sections of the educated, middle classes of Pakistan over the past 10 years. Local feminists in Pakistan do not view this as a positive development. Indeed, when I presented the findings of the first phase of this research to the WEMC inception phase meeting in Hong Kong in December 2007 to an audience of women activists from Iran, Pakistan, China and Indonesia, friends from both Iran and Pakistan were not comfortable with my analysis. One Pakistani friend angrily responded, "I find it very strange that you are portraying veiling as an empowering strategy when we in Pakistan have been fighting for years against male control over women's bodies in the name of religion."

This sentiment mirrored my own initial reaction when I moved to the UK in 2006 and started this research project. However, at the end of this journey, I have come to appreciate and understand that veiling in the UK, as in many other minority contexts is inextricably linked with the politics of anti-racism, government policies of social cohesion and integration and the search for identity in an increasingly polarised world.

I have formed invaluable friendships in the process and am grateful to the participants for sharing their viewpoints with me with such candidness, and in doing so, helping me offload some of my own intellectual baggage and escape my preconceived notions.

This is the first, evidence-based book in the United Kingdom on the issue of Muslim women's dress with a critical analysis of the debates in Britain and Europe. Lack of resources prevented me from pursuing some of the issues highlighted in greater detail, and Chapter 2 identifies some of the limitations of the methodology adopted. As such, I hope this book serves as a useful starting point for more informed debate and dialogue on this matter and will play some role in stopping the knee-jerk reactions to veiling practices that we so often hear. Equally, my intention in writing this book is to promote more measured, evidence-based academic inquiry into this important, contemporary social and political concern.

Chapter 2: Methodology

This project was conducted over a two year period from August 2006 to December 2008. This study was initiated as part of the dress code discourse and sexuality research program of the Women Living Under Muslim Laws network (WLUML) and was conceptualised as part of the WLUML component of the multi-country Women's Empowerment in Muslim Contexts (WEMC) research consortium that provided conceptual guidance and support. However, since research could not be supported from existing WEMC funds, WLUML secured a grant from the Network for Social Change to ensure that this timely research could be conducted. Without the generous support of the Network for Social Change who believed in the importance of this research for Britain, this book would not have been possible.

The first phase, from August 2006 to December 2006, involved conducting a comprehensive review of the extensive literature on the issue of Muslim women's dress in Britain. As well as consulting mainstream publications (books, newspapers and magazines), community newsletters and material from Muslim book stores in London were sourced, and a survey of literature available on the Internet was undertaken. A number of audio and visual media were also consulted. Some informal field research was conducted in this phase. The inception phase helped to identify and lay the groundwork for more intensive investigation into some key issues to be explored. A full list of these sources can be found in the Bibliography.

The second phase, from October 2007 to December 2008, consisted of a combination of in-depth, semi-structured interviews, focus group and informal discussions with 40 British Muslim women mainly of Pakistani origin (second and third generation). The respondent sample was the 20 to 33 years age group, over 80% of whom were based in London. All of these respondents had adopted the veil. The research methodology focused on the British Pakistani community as the largest and oldest (and possibly the most organised) Muslim community in the UK. A further justification for this focus on the British Pakistani community is that the younger generation's adoption of the veil represents a marked from the traditional dress of the older generation, the *shalwar kameez*.

Most of the interviews were conducted in London where the UK's Muslim population is concentrated. Lack of resources did not allow for interviews to be conducted in other cities. This is a limitation of the methodology adopted for this research. However, the impact on the findings is considered minimal.

City/Town	Number of Respondents	Percentage of Total Respondents
London (including suburbs)	32	80%
Birmingham	4	10%
Bradford	2	5%
Manchester	1	2.5%
Leicester	1	2.5%
Total	**40**	**100%**

The 40 interviews conducted by the author were of women between the ages of 20 and 33 years from the Pakistani community. These British-born respondents belonged to the middle and upper socio-economic classes. Approximately half of the group's parents were educated to degree level, with many holding positions in the highly-skilled labour market. The respondents themselves were well educated, some up to post-graduate degree level, and were employed in mainstream professions: the financial services, medicine, IT, etc. Twenty-one women were from the middle class, often second generation and lived in the inner-city neighbourhoods of East London or the London suburbs, such as Luton, Watford and Tooting.

To ensure accurate data collection, a conscious effort was made to reach a representative sample of research participants by accessing community events. I participated in a variety of community events including:

- two religious talks delivered at a Muslim community centre (North London);
- four different women-only *dars* and *tafseer* lessons;
- one women- and girls-only charity funfair at a Muslim girls primary school (East London);
- three Muslim match-making events (two in East London and one in Birmingham).

I also used these occasions to familiarise myself with the predominant community organisations and the community discourses on issues such as racism, education, family and marriage, the challenges of living as Muslims in a non-Muslim society and the perceptions of discrimination from mainstream society. For most women, the discussions often led to the question of balancing the expectations of their families and communities and enjoying the opportunities and entitlements offered as a consequence of their British citizenship.

An important component of the methodology over the two-year duration of this research was watching nearly 400 hours of religious television programming, broadcast on popular community television channels such as Islam Channel, Peace TV, Muslim TV, Prime TV, Q-TV. One limitation of the research is that it did not include community radio channels.

A number of male community leaders were also contacted. Those who consented to participating in this research are:

1. Sheikh Ibrahim Mogra, a British Muslim of Indian origin and a prominent, young community leader. He is the Imam ('prayer leader') of a Leicester mosque and Chair of the Mosque and Community Affairs Committee of the Muslim Council of Britain.[12] The significance of including his views in this book owes not only to his wide public profile as a regular contributor to programmes on BBC Radio Four and 'The Big Questions' on BBC One, but also to the fact that he represents an emerging generation of British imams born and brought up in the UK. Mogra was educated at Al-Azhar University, Cairo and also holds a postgraduate degree from the School of Oriental and African Studies, London.

2. Hafiz Akram, a Pakistani-born and trained imam who migrated to the UK and was serving as the Imam of the Harrow Central Mosque in North-West London in 2006. He is an important community leader for the Muslim population of Harrow and some surrounding boroughs. His successful fundraising efforts and community mobilisation have led to the development of a large, multi-storey building under construction to serve as the Harrow Central Mosque and Muslim Community Centre. He is regularly consulted at his office in the mosque, by men and women alike, for personal counselling and advice on private matters such as marriage.

3. Dr. Mohamed Fahim, Chairman and Head Imam at the mosque and Muslim Community Centre in South Woodford (North East London). A Chartered Engineer by profession, he was born and educated in Egypt where he worked for several years before migrating to England. He is a self-taught Islamic scholar and preacher. He is currently the proprietor of a residential care home for the elderly known as 'Greenmantle' in Woodford Green (Essex.) He is a fellow of Cambridge University where he is studying Muslim-Jewish relations and promoting inter-faith dialogue. A well-respected community leader, he acts as an Advisor on Muslim Affairs to the London's Metropolitan Police Service in addition to being the designated Chaplain at Pentonville prison.

There were also a number of Muslim women's groups and community organisations consulted for this project:

- Muslim Women's Sports Foundation (MWSF), established in 2001 by Ahmed Versi (editor of the *Muslim News*) to encourage Muslim women's participation in sports that would not compromise their religious beliefs. It is currently led by young British Muslim women.

- 'Live 4 U', a London-based group which offers counselling, life-coaching and personal development workshops for young British Muslim women.

- Sisters Games, a Birmingham-based organisation which provides women-only sports facilities.

(There were a number of other local women's groups who were consulted in the research and whose perspectives are captured in this book, but who did not want to be cited as research participations in this publication.)

These formal interviews varied in duration from half an hour to two hours. The questions I put to the interviewees were open-ended, affording them the opportunity to express their thoughts as freely as they wished and without restrictions.

This book also includes a survey of the landmark legal cases in the UK concerning Muslim students and teachers who challenged school administrations to allow them to wear their veil in the classroom. These court battles vividly showcase the debates which took place on this contentious issue.

The scope of the research extended to canvassing the debate around Muslim women's dress in a select number of Western European countries and Turkey, for the purpose of comparison. This effort was limited to desk research and the key findings are contained in Chapter 7. While more comprehensive studies of discourses surrounding the issue of the veil in these countries necessitates further research, it is hoped that the experience of the UK can shed light on some of the nuances of this complex debate.

One of the limitations of this methodology is that it did not invest in systematically mapping the responses of Muslim women-led civil society groups such as NGOs to the issue of Muslim women's dress in the UK, beyond those expressed in conferences and networking meetings. The main reason for this is that in the course of the field research, it was found that those Muslim organisations who have a faith-based membership and whose leaders observe a form of Muslim dress code widely share the views expressed by the participants of this research, which include informally organised women's groups. On the other hand, the views of those Muslim women's groups who identify themselves as secular are usually aligned with those of other feminists which are already reflected in this research.

This methodology deliberately focused on directly approaching British Muslims, both, those who veil and those who do not, and on gathering a diversity of views on veiling practices from ordinary members of the community whose voices are rarely heard but in whose name debates and policies are often formulated.

In writing this book, a careful effort has been made by the author to represent the views expressed by the participants (respondents) of the research as accurately as possible and to protect their interests. Without their willingness to share their experiences with me – which were sometimes very personal – this work would not have been possible. I would like to thank them for their time and the trust that they placed in me. In the case of any misrepresentation, it is entirely unintentional and I take full responsibility for it.

Chapter 3: A Profile of the Muslim Population of Britain

An examination of the debate on Muslim women's dress in this country should begin with a profile of Muslims in the UK. The United Kingdom of Great Britain and Northern Ireland comprises four countries: England, Northern Ireland, Scotland and Wales. Out of a total population of 58.8 million, are 1.6 million Muslims which make them the largest religious minority (at 2.8% of the total population)[13]. At least 50% of this current Muslim population was born in the UK[14]. As with previous census data, the most recent Census 2001 re-confirmed the young nature of this population with one third under 16 – the highest proportion for any group. While this Muslim population is not a homogenous unit, the vast majority come from South Asia (mainly Pakistan and Bangladesh). According to the Census 2001, there are 746,619 people in Britain of Pakistani origin (approximately 1.3% of the population) and 281,811 of Bangladeshi origin. The data collected by the Office of National Statistics shows that Pakistani Muslims are the largest ethnic group accounting for 43% of Great Britain's Muslims.

3.22 Religion[1], 2001

Millions and percentages

	Total (millions = 100%)	Percentage of people stating religion as:								
		Christian	Buddhist	Hindu	Jewish	Muslim	Sikh	Other religions	No religion	Religion not stated
North East	2.5	80.1	0.1	0.2	0.1	1.1	0.2	0.2	11.0	7.1
North West	6.7	78.0	0.2	0.4	0.4	3.0	0.1	0.2	10.5	7.2
Yorkshire and the Humber	5.0	73.1	0.1	0.3	0.2	3.8	0.4	0.2	14.1	7.8
East Midlands	4.2	72.0	0.2	1.6	0.1	1.7	0.8	0.2	15.9	7.5
West Midlands	5.3	72.6	0.2	1.1	0.1	4.1	2.0	0.2	12.3	7.5
East	5.4	72.1	0.2	0.6	0.6	1.5	0.3	0.3	16.7	7.8
London	7.2	58.2	0.8	4.1	2.1	8.5	1.5	0.5	15.8	8.7
South East	8.0	72.8	0.3	0.6	0.2	1.4	0.5	0.4	16.5	7.5
South West	4.9	74.0	0.2	0.2	0.1	0.5	0.1	0.4	16.8	7.8
England	49.1	71.7	0.3	1.1	0.5	3.1	0.7	0.3	14.6	7.7
Wales	2.9	71.9	0.2	0.2	0.1	0.8	0.1	0.2	18.5	8.1

1 Figures in this table have been adjusted to avoid the release of confidential data.

Source: Census 2001, Office for National Statistics

Like other minority religions, Muslims tend to be concentrated in particular English regions. More than a third (38%) live in London, 14% in the West Midlands, 13% in the North West and 12% in Yorkshire and the Humber.[15]

The first large-scale Muslim immigration to the UK began in the late 1950s, mostly from the Indian subcontinent, and Cyprus, following political disturbances on the island in 1957.[16]

This movement was facilitated and encouraged by the demand for import of labour by the economic boom of the post Second World War era; this labour shortage was met mostly by the inhabitants of ex-colonies of the then recently dismantled British Empire.

The British government's 1962 Commonwealth Immigration Control Act restricted migration into the UK of citizens of the British colonies and Commonwealth countries. Initially, this law prompted a rapid increase in Asian immigration as many tried to enter Britain before the ban came into effect. These immigrants built upon the community foundations created by earlier immigrants that had come largely from the Punjab and from Sylhet in East Pakistan (the region which in 1971 achieved independence as Bangladesh). Migration from Mirpur (Kashmir) accelerated in the early 1960s after the construction of the Mangla Dam in Pakistan which flooded 250 villages and displaced all their inhabitants. After the Commonwealth Control Act came into effect, nearly all new immigrants to Britain came as part of family re-unification schemes. Immigrants from East Pakistan (later Bangladesh) arrived later than those from West Pakistan (later Pakistan) and Mirpur (in Pakistan-administered Azad Kashmir).[17]

The early 1960s also witnessed a significant wave of Muslim immigrants from Africa due to the forced migration of East African Asians from countries such as Kenya and Uganda whose leaders were then pursuing Africanisation policies. These included Muslims of Pakistani, Kashmiri and Indian roots who had migrated to these countries in the late nineteenth and early twentieth centuries during British colonial rule (over the Indian sub-continent.) The initial wave of mass migration from South Asia occurred to provide the labour force for the construction of the East African railways under British rule. In time, the railway stations led to the set up of towns which provided opportunities for settlement and commerce to the migrants. The British government offered citizenship to certain nationals of its former colonies. In 1968, the Labour Government limited this practice and refused immediate right of residence to British passport holders. The policy was revised when General Idi Amin of Uganda began his persecution of Asians. In September 1972 he expelled almost all of the country's South Asian population, forcing the British government to admit large numbers of African Asians into the UK (Hunter: 2002, p.52).

During this period, smaller numbers of immigrants from Malaysia, Morocco, and Yemen arrived in the UK. The late 1970s and early 1980s also saw an influx of Iranians, mostly refugees from the new Islamic Republic. Members of political dissident groups from Arab countries or members of communities who were under pressure by their own governments, such as Shi'i Muslims from Iraq, also came to Britain during the 1980s. Thousands of Algerian refugees fleeing the unrest in Algeria sought asylum in the UK beginning in 1992. These successive waves of Muslim migrants, caused by different geo-political realities, created a British Muslim community comprising many ethnic, cultural and sectarian groups. Its members differ in terms of their level of education, socio-economic status, political participation, retentions of links to home countries and their involvement in 'Muslim activism'.

The Pakistani diaspora, as the numerically strongest ethnic group, is usually at the forefront of Muslim activism in Britain. The majority belong to the canal colonies[18] of the Punjab province and Azad Kashmir (Pakistan-administered Kashmir). Most of the early migrants from the rural areas of these regions came to the UK in the 1960s when the introduction of the Green Revolution forced many out of the rural labour market. These first-generation migrants found subsistence as blue-collar workers in British factories facing a shortage of manual labour. The initial migration of men was followed by that of women from villages in Pakistan, who over time joined their husbands, allowing for the permanent settlement of these communities in the UK.

The decades following the 1960s also witnessed a large number of highly educated professionals from Pakistan's upper-middle and upper classes settling in England. Many men from the Pakistani élite went to Britain to pursue higher education and remained there on completion of their studies. The low wages in Pakistan, and lack of professional development opportunities as well as political instability, as civilian rule was periodically interrupted by martial law, were factors in the decision of many to remain in the UK. In short, their new lifestyle expectations and the individual freedoms they experienced in Britain were perceived as missing in the home country.

Today, 46% of the British Muslim population are British-born and 33% are under 16. As a faith group, some socio-economic indicators show them lagging behind: 36% of British Muslims leave school without qualifications. British Muslims are also a faith group which stands out for having the highest unemployment rate: 17% of all Muslim men of working age in England and Wales and 18% of all Muslim women of working age. As a comparison, the national average for unemployment in the same year was 6% for men and 5% for women of working age. The data quoted in this paragraph was obtained from the 2001 Census published by the Office of National Statistics.

Chapter 4: Identity Assertion or Divide and Rule?

4.1 Evolution of Muslim Community Activism

Arguably, the term 'Muslim community' is misleading as it disregards the plurality of ethnic and cultural backgrounds which British Muslims today represent: Somali, Pakistani, Iranian, Bangladeshi, Indian, Turkish, Afghan and Arab. Nevertheless, the fact that these Muslims from such diverse backgrounds have over the years come together on inclusive institutional platforms such as the Muslim Council of Britain (MCB) is indicative of their willingness to increasingly promote themselves and their interests under a homogenous 'Muslim' identity. To a large extent, this is also a response to Britain's policy of multiculturalism as a means of encouraging integration of immigrants and social cohesion where numerical strength counts in competing for state concessions, lobbying and resources. Thus, immigrants belonging to the Islamic faith can experience a far greater strength under a collective identity as Muslims rather than constituent ethnic groups as Pakistani, Iranian or Bangladeshi.

Equally important here is the role of discrimination experienced by British Muslims in their interaction with the host population (Nielsen: 1992, p.14). Whereas discrimination or racism was earlier contested by 'Asians' (Hindus, Sikhs and Muslims) who organised collectively – based on their common experience of labour – to fight for their rights in 1960s and 1970s Britain, racism was subsequently negotiated by faith groups representing each faith community. This was in large part due to the weakening of trade unionism and the Labour Party's move to the centre as well as the result of transnational organizing by conservative politico-religious groups as they expanded their constituencies within western liberal democracies. The result was a steady transfer of power from ethnic community associations (including professional associations) as legitimate community representatives and interest groups to organisations increasingly adopting a religious character and claiming legitimacy of community representation explicitly on the basis of religion. As memories of the country of origin eroded among the second and third generations, greater emphasis was laid on religious consciousness as the common factor binding each community. The second generation has no memory of their parents' country of origin – for them, Britain 'is home'.

As Muslims of various ethnic backgrounds settled into their lives as British citizens, and at a time when the British government cut funding to anti-racist organisations, they found common ground on issues of appropriate education for their children, building of mosques, provision of *halal* food, etc. Their organisation into formal groups and institutions was galvanised by key events from the 1980s onwards: the Salman Rushdie affair, demands for Religious Education (curriculum in state schools) to include basic teaching about Islam, *halal* meals in schools and school uniforms (to comply with their interpretation of modesty). These issues were instrumental in mobilising small Muslim institutions to build larger alliances across the country to secure concessions from local government (for instance, the local council). Many significant demands were met such as the demand for Islamic faith schools and separate Islamic schools for girls in places like Bradford and Birmingham. Thus education became a focal point for the beginnings of Muslim community activism in Britain. Mosque leaders proposed faith schools as a solution to racism faced by Muslim children in mainstream schools and to ensure appropriate education to British Muslim children which would make them conscious of their religious values.

The Rushdie affair is widely remembered as a turning point in the history (and the beginning) of early British Muslim community activism. While it was certainly a catalyst, there were other factors at play which created an environment conducive to this transition to faith-based politics from anti-racism campaigning. The UK government's response to the anti-racist demonstrations and the race riots was to adopt a policy of multiculturalism which celebrated difference and redefined racism not just as a denial of equal rights but as also the denial of the right to be different. Under this policy, people of other ethnicities did not need to accept 'British values'. On the surface, this seems like a fair approach but it is ridden with complexities and has resulted in a culture of self-censorship for fear of offending an identity group. It has prevented many British Muslim women from resisting and openly challenging the patriarchal barriers erected in their own communities that are defended in the name of religion.

Dubbing this as the 'politics of difference', the writer, lecture and activist, Kenan Malik writes:

> Multiculturalism transformed the character of antiracism. By the mid-1980s the focus of antiracist protest in Bradford had shifted from political issues, such as policing and immigration, to religious and cultural issues: a demand for Muslim schools and for separate education for girls, a campaign for *halal* meat to be served at school, and, most explosively, the confrontation over the publication of *The Satanic Verses*. Political struggles unite across ethnic or cultural divisions; cultural struggles inevitably fragment. As different groups began asserting their particular identities ever more fiercely, so the shift from the political to the cultural arena helped to create a more tribal city.

Secular Muslims were regarded as betraying their culture (they belonged to the 'white left') while radical Islam became not just more acceptable but, too many, more authentic.

This process was strengthened by a new relationship between the local council and the local mosques. In 1981, the council helped set up and fund the Bradford Council of Mosques and looked to it as a voice of the community. This helped marginalise secular radicals - the Asian Youth Movement eventually broke up - and allowed religious leaders to reassert their power. As the secular tradition was squeezed out, the only place offering shelter for disaffected youth was militant Islam.

Multiculturalism did not create militant Islam, but it helped create a space for it within British Muslim communities that had not existed before. It fostered a more tribal nation, undermined progressive trends within the Muslim communities and strengthened the hand of conservative religious leaders - all in the name of antiracism.[19]

It should, however, be remembered that this policy of multiculturalism was not one that was demanded by the minorities. The anti-racism campaigners concentrated on gaining political equality and struggled against discriminatory immigration controls, racist attacks and police brutality. They also spoke against some traditional values and the dominance of the mosque and were concerned about improving the status of women.

The participation of women in early Muslim community organisation was not visible. While many British Asian men who were engaged in secular, anti-racist and sometimes even leftist political campaigns joined Muslim associations after the Rushdie Affair, women activists did not. As Rahila Gupta, a member of the prominent, anti-racist women's group, Southall Black Sisters recalls:

The contradictions arising from WAF's (Women Against Fundamentalisms) position of resisting racism, sexism and religious fundamentalism were perfectly demonstrated by the WAF picket outside parliament in 1989 – approximately 50 women were marooned between a march of young Asian men calling for a ban on *The Satanic Verses* and National Front (NF) supporters. Instead of tackling the NF, the Asian men verbally and physically attacked WAF which then had to rely on the police for protection whereas previously WAF members would have been marching alongside their Asian 'brothers' against police and state racism!

The fallout from the Rushdie affair was the widespread growth of religious identities at the expense of racial and gender identities. Secular anti-racists began to declaim, even reclaim, their Muslim identity. Muslim women increasingly adopted the hijab as a symbol of pride in their religious identity, not recognising or even accepting the fact that it set women back by placing the onus on women's safety or their modest dress and behaviour rather than male aggression. The left displayed a reluctance to challenge reactionary forces within our communities because it might be seen as racist.[20]

In recent years, the most vocal Muslim institutions have enjoyed the widespread support of British Muslims who appreciate, in particular, their role in negotiating with the Government to defend their civil liberties. This is especially true of the post-9/11 and 7/7[21] world where Muslim youth have been subjected to stop-and-search policies taken as part of anti-terrorism procedures enforced by the authorities. These policies once again led to the expansion of alliances and networks among Muslim organisations that spoke on behalf of the Muslim communities against Britain's foreign policy and openly held the country's stance on Iraq, the Palestinian-Israeli conflict and Afghanistan responsible for the growing anger and alienation among the British Muslim youth. The post-7/7 context also led to a further mushrooming of (Islamic) identity-based groups who capitalised on the Government's search for domestic Muslim allies in its 'war on terrorism'. These new groups may have a 'moderate' stance on issues of public order, but are perhaps not so progressive on the question of women's rights.

Indeed, many Muslim community organisations have benefited from significant funding, as well as from increased access to spheres of power, as the British Government sought alliances in the name of combating terrorism. Inevitably, this has caused friction and a loosening of inter-faith and inter-ethnic alliances as Hindu and other faith groups compete for similar state financing. Under Britain's policy of multiculturalism, local councils and government authorities cannot discriminate between faith groups and are obliged to provide proportional funding to each community.

Many civil society groups have questioned what they see as the official compartmentalisation of British citizens into distinct religious communities, causing divisions between faith groups rather than promoting cohesion.

Muslim groups seeking to justify their privileged position respond to this criticism by arguing that they have opened the path for other faith groups to access more government funding and this competition for resources will strengthen other faith communities as well. Since 7/7, with all the attention focused on the British Muslim communities, there emerged demands for resources for empowering and improving the situation of British Muslim women as key allies in preventing violent extremism. This was based on the recognition that women's voices were seldom heard and their viewpoints seldom represented by the Muslim community groups whose leadership is predominantly male. As a result, some new Muslim women's groups have been formed in recent years.

One such recently formed group is the National Muslim Women's Advocacy Group (NMWAG), led by 19 Muslim women, of whom seven are based in London, which represents a wide spectrum of communities, professions and traditions. NMWAG was formed to advise Government on the role that they can play in 'winning hearts and minds and tackling extremism'. It was launched by the Government, and the Communities Secretary, Hazel Blears, chaired its first meeting on 21 November 2007.

The specific remit of the group is to:
- act as ambassadors for Muslim women at the grassroots level and represent their views and concerns to Government;
- provide leadership to communities and act as positive role models for Muslim women in society;
- empower Muslim women to engage more with the media on a wide range of issues and help dispel myths around the role of Muslim women in society;
- meet in the form of a round table to discuss issues and concerns that are affecting Muslim women, e.g. access for women in mosques.[22]

NMWAG seems to meet the need of the hour for British Muslim women, and indeed the carefully selected membership of the group could possibly (at least in the short term) help to shape a more progressive agenda committed to increasing options for British Muslim women[23]. Nevertheless, the broader question of the perception of groups such as NMWAG and the recently established Young Muslims Advisory Group (YMAG) among other communities and wider society merits some reflection. Does the creation of such groups, promoted by the Government, reflect a failure of Britain's policy of multiculturalism in so far as it can be considered to have an adverse effect on social cohesion?

The Government's actions in promoting these Muslim institutions are provoking resentment among other minority faith groups such as Hindus. This was evident in the remarks of a Hindu councillor at a local borough meeting in early 2009 attended by the author. The meeting brought together Muslim women to form a network and consultation about how the Council could better respond to the needs of the Muslim women resident in the borough. The aforementioned councillor, who cannot be identified for reasons of confidentiality, questioned her colleagues' decision openly and asked why other Asian women were not invited. She was of the opinion that none of the concerns raised by the workshop participants were exclusively 'Muslim' demands.

Even if other faith groups were to become similarly successful in negotiating concessions and securing funding from the Government, what would it mean for Britain's social fabric? What would Britain's multicultural map look like if we have a National Hindu Muslim Women's Group, a Jewish Women's Group and a Christian Women's Group? Would this erode the precious gains of the joint labour struggles and the BME movement of the 1970s? Would it silence the secular British women who are part of each of these communities? Would it lead to the selective enforcement of religion as the main marker of identity in Britain? Are British Muslim women's concerns really so different from those of other British women?

This sentiment is echoed in the comments of the Conservative Party Shadow Cabinet Minister for Social Cohesion, Baroness Sayeeda Warsi. Responding to questions in the House of Lords soon after the creation of the NMWAG, she said:

> The creation of such groups is actually dividing communities and it is quite patronising because it says to Muslim women you can only engage with us as Muslim women and not as individuals.

Defending the Labour Government, Lord Patel of Bradford responded to this criticism as follows:

> If it is suggested that by focusing on Muslims or Muslim women we are patronising them or creating divisions that were not previously there I completely disagree. We are working with a community that has disproportionately high rates of unemployment, poor educational attainment

and poor health all of which lead to disenfranchisement and alienation. We cannot address those issues if we don't engage with them just as we do with wider inter-faith groups.[24]

The challenge therefore is: will Muslim women and the larger Muslim community successfully use this official patronage for the betterment of Muslim women and increase options for them while also improving social cohesion?

The immediate rationale for establishing NMWAG and providing funding to similar 'moderate' groups of hand-picked individuals lies in the 'preventing violent extremism' agenda of the British Government, which it developed post-9/11. In fact, it is clear that had the terrorist attacks of 9/11 and 7/7 not occurred, NMWAG and YMAG and several other groups would not exist today.

Taking a longer historical perspective, while these partnerships have gained momentum since 9/11, they can also be considered a continuation of Britain's policy of liberal multiculturalism; for the past two decades the Government has enshrined community politics through new partnership structures. In this form of governance, the link between the British Government and its Muslim subjects is increasingly mediated through the mosque and other faith-based organisations (Glynn: 2008, p.2) to the exclusion of other forms of civil society organizing.

Against this background, the terrorist attacks of 7/7 only seem to have precipitated the desire of Tony Blair's New Labour Government to establish alliances with acceptable ('moderate') groups, of which more could be created if there were not enough. Britain has witnessed an intense debate in recent years about the definition of the 'moderate' Muslim. Many in British Muslim communities distrust the motivations of the Government in rewarding and forming alliances with 'moderate' groups and its 'Prevent Violent Extremism' agenda. Many British newspaper column inches have been given over to determining the profile of the 'moderate' Muslim. In general, what seems acceptable to the British Government is a Muslim who backs British foreign and domestic policies, espouses 'western values', and does not believe in violent protest. To further propagate the notion of 'moderate Muslims', in 2007, the Secretary of State for Communities and Local Government set up a theology board of Muslim scholars and community leaders "to lead thinking on Islam in a modern context". The board is meant to discuss issues affecting British Muslims such as "what it means to be Muslim in the UK in the 21st century", a Muslim's loyalty to Britain and women's rights in Islam. In order to disseminate its message the body is expected to organise seminars across the country to promote a peaceful vision of Islam and engage the wider Muslim community in the debate as well.

Returning to the discussion of Britain's multiculturalism, while the Conservative Party previously supported a policy of multiculturalism – having backed the creation of the Muslim Council of Britain – it has subsequently retreated from this position. It now considers multiculturalism a thing of the past. Commenting on the creation of the Young Muslims Advisory Group, the Shadow Minister for Community Cohesion, Baroness Sayeeda Warsi said:

> This is another example of the government engaging with the British Muslim communities on the basis purely of their faith. There are many issues that face young people: drugs, unemployment and housing, to name but a few.

> To select a group of twenty two young people, however talented they may be, to advise the government on 'Muslim issues' is patronising and deeply concerning.

> When will the Government learn that the Muslim community is not a homogenous block, and the issues its young people face are predominantly the same issues that all young people in this country face, whatever their background, race, or religion?

> Actions such as this are a continuation of the Government's policy of state multiculturalism, which creates a more divided Britain.[25]

Researcher Sarah Glynn aptly articulates the challenges faced in this brand of state multiculturalism as follows:

> The promotion of faith groups of all kinds and the emphasis on a person's religious affiliation is helping to consolidate the power of religious organisations and foreground religious identity. The official argument that the incorporation of faith-based bodies contributes to 'social cohesion' and that 'Muslim identity politics can support and encourage integration' seems, at best, naïve, if not dangerously sophistic. Religious mobilisation may, indeed, encourage participation in the political process, and many Islamic groups do encourage their followers to become exemplary members of civil society. However, they become involved first and foremost as Muslims and

the government approach seems designed to perpetuate and institutionalise their religious difference. Faith groups may see a mutual benefit in such a system… but anything that highlights Muslim difference and especially that appears to be giving special support for Muslims as Muslims is likely to generate a negative reaction in the wider population. More broadly, too… the promotion of religious organisations is being used by neoliberal regimes as an important method of social control, through a combination of social conservatism, strong hierarchical organisation and the colonial practice of divide and rule. This must be of concern to anyone hoping for the development of a more progressive position to neo-liberalism.[26]

Some young British Muslims have also raised concerns about the legitimacy of these organisations' claims to represent or speak on behalf of British Muslim communities. Many (secular, feminist) women are worried about their influence on the Muslim communities as they propagate views on defining women's role in society according to their favoured (selective) interpretations of Islam. These definitions range from education and etiquette to dress.

4.2 British Muslim Women in Community Activism

Contrary to popular perception, women's receptiveness to veiling practices should not be mistaken for any measure of passivity or reluctance to participate in the public sphere. Indeed the very fact that they are visible in the workforce and also in promoting the veil themselves contradicts the assumption that veiled women are by default oppressed.

One such effort where Muslim women have increasingly challenged traditional gender roles and male authority was launched during the course of this research. It involved public advocacy work to open mosques to women for regular prayers rather than on Fridays and special occasions only, and to turn mosques into vibrant community centres. This campaign was launched in October 2006, by the Muslim Public Affairs Committee UK[27] (MPACUK) women's team, most of whom wore at least a *hijab* themselves if not the *jilbab* or *niqab*, who distributed dossiers to members of the public quoting a *hadith* regarding positive and supportive views on women's participation in the mosque[28].

This campaign, which featured in a Channel 4 television documentary entitled 'Women Only Jihad', was groundbreaking insofar as it publicly and loudly raised British Muslim women's demand to access the mosque and to have a regular, clean area of the prayer hall dedicated to them. MPACUK women activists also demanded that women should be included in the Mosque Management Committee as equal stakeholders of the community and users of the mosque. They justified these demands by quoting examples of the Prophet's wife Aisha (RA) who was closely involved in advising the Prophet's companions and in mosque affairs. However, judging from the hundreds of comments on the MPACUK website, as well as the response of the Muslim men using the mosques, the imams and management committees that are captured in the documentary, there is still a long way to go before British Muslim women are able to participate in the management of mosques.

These demands were earlier heard from prominent Muslim women in a meeting at 10 Downing Street with the Prime Minister, Tony Blair on 10 May 2006:

> Women and young people are excluded from mosque committees. Giving them the opportunity to be on a board could lead to more women and young Muslims getting involved in politics and public life.

> Women should be encouraged to play a greater part in the running of mosques by being allowed to join committees etc. The role of Imams is crucial in this regard, as the messages they give are key to what people believe. However, some women feel they cannot get past the taboo of entering mosques and find it difficult to speak directly to the Imam.[29]

Erica Timoney (associated with the New Muslims Project of the Islamic Foundation in Leicester), attending the meeting, told the Prime Minister that, "There are some mosques that don't allow Muslim women through the doors, whilst others don't have any women in their committees. Exclusion from grassroots committees means they [women] don't have the springboard to political life." The forty women attending the meeting looked to the Government for support to tackle this problem on the grounds of sexual discrimination.

The participants went a step further to call for greater monitoring of mosques which is a far cry from the demands ever made by any Muslim (men-led) institution: "Mosques should be made accountable to the Government – people should be able to make a complaint about a mosque to a local government committee or officer."

These examples illustrate the way in which British Muslim women have used their own religious identity to challenge gender stereotypes that cast them as being passive within the community. Far from being mere recipients of ideology, they are using the framework of Islam to advocate for a greater role in decision-making even in what have typically been considered male domains. They seem to have embarked on a twin strategy of using 'western' arguments of sex discrimination to gain state support in their struggle for inclusion in Muslim decision-making tiers and relying on Islam itself to garner community support for their stance.

As Humera Khan, founding member of the An-Nisa Women's Society in Brent (London) said,

> More women are realizing the cost of being absent from the circles of Muslim power. We are far more well-informed and politicised than men realise. If they don't tap into our insights, they will go round in circles with a lop-sided approach to community development.[30]

British Muslim women, including those subscribing to dress codes deemed Muslim, are trying to find a place for themselves in the leadership of Muslim organisations. Presently, their role in these organisations is inadequate as they remain limited to what they view as women's affairs defined in exclusive 'sisters committees'. They are seldom part of the strategic steering committees of the best-known and largest of these institutions, which hold the view that the public arena is not chaste or appropriate for pious women. It is in this context that MPACUK's call for inclusion of women in mosque affairs is labelled as 'Women Only Jihad'.

This call for reclaiming women's space in the mosque is not unique to the UK. In Canada, a Muslim woman journalist and filmmaker, Zarqa Nawaz, launched a similar initiative through her 2005 documentary entitled 'Me and the Mosque'. 'Me and the Mosque' was supported by the National Film Board of Canada in partnership with CBC Newsworld. Zarqa Nawaz is a second-generation Canadian Muslim, born to Pakistani immigrants in Toronto. Her documentary is an account of her travels across Canada to visit mosques and explore the historical role of women in Islam and the barriers set up in Canadian mosques in recent years to segregate women from men. It features personal stories of anger, fear, acceptance and defiance of young Canadian Muslim women about these barriers[31].

The scholar, Amina Wadud (a convert to Islam) took this a step further when she led a Friday prayer of over a hundred male and female Muslims in the Episcopal Cathedral of St. John the Divine in New York, on 18 March 2005. Since then, she has continued to lead prayers on various occasions and has hence been the subject of much debate.

Whether it is about claiming access to public space for women or involvement in decision making and community affairs, women's legitimacy in getting their voice heard is reportedly closely linked to observance of what is perceived as a modest dress code. According to a leading British Muslim woman activist from London engaged in championing British Muslim women's representation in public life, Muslims are using the veil to carve out a space for themselves in organised community activism which has traditionally been dominated by men. The source, who was interviewed for this research, but who wishes to remain anonymous and who is no stranger to the corridors of power, revealed that the emphasis on *hijab* by the Muslim community is such that in order to win credibility to sit among *ulema* and deliberate on theological issues, she has to wear the headscarf and appropriate clothing:

> Although they say that *hijab* is a matter of personal choice, they will not engage with women who do not wear it. I know that if I don't cover my head, access will be denied because chastity is defined by them in how much a woman is covered.

She reported that apart from her high-level meetings with male (Muslim) community leaders and other public speaking events where she consciously covers her head, this was evident at the London Muslim Centre where "*hijab* is very much the dress code."[32]

She believes that these unspoken rules mean that "dress codes are being used to disengage with women... it's like a baton for beating women who are working outside the box." She insisted that concern with the *hijab* is very much an "internal Muslim community issue" while the more hotly contested issue for the wider society is the *niqab*, as the latter is widely perceived as a physical barrier to communication (and security) as it conceals a person's identity.

Nevertheless, it would not be accurate to state that all Muslim women (especially those who observe some sort of veil) are equally frustrated with their under-representation in the leadership of these institutions. Indeed, many firmly endorse their role in community development and women's only youth projects and religious instruction (*tafseer* and *dars*) sections as appropriate forums for engagement in conformity with their religious beliefs. They do not consider themselves oppressed for conducting these meetings in the safety and comfort of their own homes. Indeed, many newcomers who adopt the veil and participate in these discussions find themselves motivated to be more pro-active in arranging fundraisers for

Muslim charities and even feel empowered in setting the boundaries or terms of such engagement themselves.

They proudly attend Islamic talks, discussions and (Muslim) community events. These platforms serve a pivotal role in their eagerness to educate themselves about religion. For instance, 'Live 4 U' is a group run by two sisters (converts to Islam from Hinduism) in East London. Both women work as full-time personal assistants in the corporate sector, but as self-proclaimed 'reverts' to Islam, they decided to set up a small business organisation called 'Live 4 U' offering life coaching and counselling for personal development to Muslim women. Both types of services are offered from within their interpretation of an Islamic framework. While their two-day workshop (on life coaching) touched upon sources of personal happiness where participants had to rate their level of self-satisfaction against different aspects of their lives (career, money, health, love and romance), the solution the workshop promoted was finding motivation through Islamic instruction. For example, at the end of the first day, the two-week 'Daily Deeds/Character Checklist' which each participant had to report against had the following criteria: 'wake up for Fajr', 'Salaam a Sister', 'Refrain from a bad act' and 'Perform all Salaah/Namaaz'. How such groups promote specific modes of dress can be judged by their logo alone which features a faceless woman wearing a headscarf. (Whether this endorsement is done intentionally or unintentionally remains unclear, yet in the case of 'Live 4 U' both trainers and participants clearly defined veiling as a religious duty.) While the question of dress did not form part of any (formal) exercise, it came up within the first hour of discussion from participants complaining about the difficulty of continuing to wear their veils in public (of the six participants, four wore the *jilbab*, one wore a *niqab* with the *jilbab* and one wore only a *hijab*). When discussing how to spread the *deen* ('religion') and educate women about the religion, one of the trainers recommended:

> If someone is not wearing *hijab*, if the person is not ready, then don't insult them. Encourage them but don't force it. As long as the message is given, your deed is done. Remember that God's delays are not God's denials.

However, one participant, Farzana Chaudhry from Walthamstow insisted that "some people need a bit of a push to cover their head… I think if we give that push, it's alright. When I started wearing the *jilbab* and *niqab*, I used to call my best friend every few days to tell her how much of a difference it made in my life. She didn't used to like hearing it but after a few months, she called me one day and said 'I've started covering my head and it's because of you'. So a gentle push in the right direction might just make your friends thank you. After all, it is our duty to look after the best interests of our fellow Muslims and to guide them to the right path. If we tell our friends to cover their heads, we have their best interest in our hearts. Allah *subhanatallah* says that convincing people to the right path is very difficult but it is very rewarding. We must remain steadfast in our belief."[33]

Farzana's sentiments echoed those of other participants in the room who all nodded their heads in agreement. They were convinced that it was their duty to preach and proselytise as this was what they understood would make God happy.

The appeal of such grassroots organisations lies in the sense of solidarity which participants feel as Muslims. One of them, twenty-six year old data analyst, Mona Irfan excitedly invited me to attend a lecture at the Abrar Islamic Foundation in central London saying, "You should come, you'll really like them. I met load of sisters over there!" (M. Irfan, personal communication, 1 September 2006)

This enthusiasm stems from deep convictions and positive experiences at a personal level, but it can also be linked to broader strategies pursued by advocates of political Islam. From Sri Lanka to Indonesia and Mali to Egypt, individual believers are encouraged to 'spread the word' and to persuade others to join 'the community', thereby strengthening both its reach and its overall political power. An individual's search – for community, support, answers, absolute truth – then becomes an effective mean to serve a collective, political, agenda.

These forums are considered as an empowering experience where they discuss and learn about finding solutions to their everyday problems through Islamic teachings. Addressing each other as 'brothers' or 'sisters', they share a sense of solidarity which transcends the cultural divide as far as their origins are concerned. Of particular importance to respondents were topics on women's role in family and society. Twenty-eight year old Raheema Abbas said that she normally attended these lectures by (male) scholars (where men and women sit separately but in the same room) on Islamic guidelines on choosing a spouse, working in a mixed environment and parenting. These topics reflect women's concerns (with a focus on marriage and motherhood), while at the same time emphasizing gender roles as justified by a set of religious prescriptions.

Another aspect in which women were engaged was in they eagerly volunteering for fundraising roles for Muslim charities with outreach in Muslim countries across the world, such as Islamic Relief, Muslim Aid and Muslim Hands. Popular forums included the City Circle[34], the Muslim Professionals UK[35], the Muslim World

League, Utruijj and numerous websites. Participation in these events encouraged respondents to become more involved in public life.

Gatherings like these also inevitably provide an acceptable space for young people to find prospective marriage partners. Rejecting the western concept of dating as un-Islamic and the traditional preference for arranged marriage as stifling individual freedom, the younger generation has come up with innovative ways of what is sometimes described as 'Islamic dating.' In their search for a 'decent Muslim' girl or boy, young people are exercising personal choice in choosing their spouse within what they define as Islamic parameters by going on chaperoned dates or arranging meetings with the mediation of mutual friends.

Taking their role even further, many community leaders are now organising Muslim marriage events to facilitate partnerships between young Muslims in an atmosphere within the bounds of what is deemed Islamic by them. These events are becoming very popular; at least two or three are held every month in one of the major cities of England. Most events are free of charge – particularly those held within a Muslim community centre. There are also events where attendees have to pay a registration fee of between £5 and £60. Two such gatherings were attended by the author for the purposes of this research: one in Birmingham and one in London. Both events had a similar agenda: a half-hour talk or lecture by an Islamic scholar or imam, a one-hour ice-breaking session with group work, refreshments and the opportunity to mingle with members of the opposite sex. The main difference between the two events was that while the invitation for the one in Birmingham strongly encouraged participants to come accompanied by a *mahram*, with parents or siblings to 'facilitate', the London event was open to participants only. Justifying these admission criteria, thirty-three year old Nadia Bushra who co-organised the event with Dr. Mohammed Fahim said that the exclusion of parents was necessary to allow young people to freely discuss their concerns and approach anyone they chose. She added that when parents accompany their children they tend to guide them towards only those they deem suitable. She said,

> Pakistani parents want their daughters and sons to only marry Pakistanis, and Afghanis want to marry only Afghanis. But this is not a realistic demand – living in Britain, we already have a very small Muslim community and when you force such preferences, you are limiting the pool even more… Finding a suitable partner is such a huge concern in the community so we thought of providing this safe space to youngsters…it is a forum where they can meet each other and discuss. They don't need a *mahram* here because

the Imam is present and we are sitting in a mosque altogether. (N. Bushra, personal communication, 13 April 2008)

Nadia Bushra volunteers at the Muslim Community Centre and Mosque in South Woodford and was the main driver behind these events. The first gathering was held in December 2007.

On the other hand, the event in Birmingham while requiring *mahrams*, also specified the dress code on the invitation as 'smart/casual but modest.' It was organised by the Islamic Circles, a London-based organisation which runs an ongoing, popular project called 'Muslim Marriage Events' across England. This event required prior registration and submission of a profile of each participant which was on display on site. Islamic Circles organises many such events every month and often for select audiences within the Muslim community. For example, they offer specific events catering only to 'doctors', 'converts to Islam', 'Canary Wharf Muslim Professionals', 'Turkish Muslims', 'Gujrati Muslims', etc[36].

These informal networks of women, which provide them an alternative and parallel form of empowerment, reflect the ethnic diversity of the Muslim population itself. Their increasing willingness to participate in these Muslim networks and to use them to challenge Muslim men's monopoly over religion and over defining women's role in the name of Islam is indicative of their agency. Through these networks, they also work on issues to which they themselves attach importance.

Nevertheless, women remain severely excluded from national level politics, while having some representation at the council level in local government. There is only one Muslim woman Member of Parliament in the House of Lords and there is none at the House of Commons. As Muslim women want to be heard and consulted by the Government on issues relevant to their community, they need to focus on increasing their representation in Parliament in order to influence policy-making.

4.3 Proliferation of Dress Codes Ideology

On the issue of Muslim women's dress, there is a wide range of websites, DVDs and publications advocating varying degrees of veiling for Muslim women. Books on these issues are available at most Islamic centres as well as community bookshops. Titles include *The Hijab, Dress for Every Muslimah – An Encouragement and Clarification*[37], *Adornment of Women in Forensic and Medical Perspective*[38] and *The Obligation of Veiling*[39]. The back cover of the book recommends the *hijab* as follows:

We as Muslim sisters must remember that the Hijab is one of our means of getting into Paradise. We should feel honoured and dignified. We should feel protected, secure and obedient. We should feel guarded like a pearl. In Paradise, everyone will have eternal youth and never get old and enjoy what they like forever.

It is worth noting that the debate in the UK is influenced by broader political contexts, brought to light by the fact several of the authors are from Saudi Arabia, a country where strict dress codes for women is heavily influenced by *Wahhabism*.

The Islamic Foundation UK has even printed a book for young children called, *I Can Wear Hijab Anywhere!*[140] With the aid of colourful illustrations, the book promotes the *hijab* as a 'norm' and an 'Islamic prescription' for girls and women, and seeks to encourage young girls to wear it. Illustrations show veiled girls (wearing loose, long shirts, trousers and a *hijab*) in clearly recognisable British settings – riding a traditional black taxi, the Big Bus (Sightseeing Tour of London), visiting the London Zoo and playing outdoor games. It seeks to show that far from being incompatible with 'British values', the *hijab* represents and embraces modernity.

Not all British Muslim women and men agree with the veiling of pre-pubescent girls. Indeed, there is much concern about this practice that is on the increase. Critics condemn it on two grounds. Firstly, that imposing the *hijab* on girls as young as four-years old is tantamount to imposing a sexuality or a sexual appeal on these children where it does not or should not exist. Secondly, that enforcing it on girls at such a young age is in fact denying them the freedom of choice as individuals[41]. Nevertheless, it must be said that this practice is not necessarily encouraged by imams, some of whom consider it to contradict the spirit of Islam and to be unjust as Islam does not require *veiling* for pre-pubescent girls[42].

Similarly, there are many programmes and talk shows hosted by women on Muslim community channels such as the Islam Channel which promote 'modest' attire for girls. They are actively using the media for public advocacy on important issues facing British Muslims. For instance, the regular weekly programme, 'Muslimah Dilemma' on the Islam Channel, frequently has coverage of young Muslim girls' and women's youth support groups and projects. A new talk show launched on the Channel in 2008, 'City Sister', features a group of four of five guests and a presenter discussing issues such as how to find a prospective marriage partner, how to dress as a Muslim woman, etc. Islam Channel stands out as the community channel with the most viewers among the British Muslim community. This positions the channel as a very influential media player; its role in promoting Muslim veils is important – all its female presenters and reporters wear either a *hijab* or a *jilbab* including all those presenting children's programmes. The Islam Channel's official website also features two video clips of two female presenters demonstrating the different styles of wearing the *hijab*[43].

The average person in the UK does not understand why Muslim women are increasingly adopting different forms of Muslim dress, with a recent poll showing some 33% of the population in favour of a ban on the face-veil.[44] What motivates British Muslim women to adopt the veil despite this hostile environment merits deeper scrutiny.

There is tremendous diversity among the various forms of Muslim dress prevalent not only in the UK but around the world. This diversity and associated interpretations of modesty are often overlooked in polemical debates surrounding the issue. There are various types of Muslim women's dress which offer degrees of covering. For instance, the *hijab* is a type of scarf wrapped around the head which covers the neck and hair but reveals the face. The *niqab*, also commonly known as the 'face veil' is a type of veil which covers the neck, hair and whole face except the wearer's eyes. There are different variations on the *niqab* which serve this purpose of covering the face. Some include fastening the cloth around the forehead and letting it fall to cover the entire face with a place cut out only for the eyes. Others are fastened over the *hijab* around the bridge of the nose so that some of the forehead is also visible.

The *jilbab* is an outer garment worn for the purpose of veiling by women. It is a long, loose-fitting coat which covers the entire body except the hands, feet, face and head. Typically, the *jilbab* is worn along with either a *hijab* or *niqab* to cover the head. It is commonly worn in Middle Eastern countries such as Saudi Arabia and the United Arab Emirates, etc. and has been adopted among sections of the British Muslim community as well.

Many first generation British Muslim women also wear the *shalwar kameez* which is a traditional dress worn by men and women across South Asia. It is also the national dress of Pakistan. Worn in many different styles, fabrics, patterns and colours, the dress consists of a shirt or tunic known as the *kameez* and a pair of trousers or pyjamas which are loose around the waist and gradually narrow towards the ankles. For women, the *shalwar kameez* is not considered complete without the *dupatta*: a large stole or shawl which is wrapped around the neck or head. By customary practice, the *dupatta* serves as the all-important symbol of modesty without which women do not step out of the house.

In Britain, there are generational differences in dress; younger women are more particular about covering their heads with specific garments such as the *hijab* compared to their mothers who were content with *shalwar kameez* and *dupattas*. This difference in dress practices signifies a significant departure from the outlook of the first generation; the second and third generation's heightened religious consciousness and education allows them to argue for gender equality, rejecting the ways in which Islam is traditionally interpreted by men. It is argued that women who wear the *hijab* are redefining the *Ummah* as more inclusive, with younger women becoming more visible and vocal, yet often within the confines of 'acceptable' dress codes.

Discussing this trend, Sheikh Ibrahim Mogra, a British educated *imam* of a Leicester mosque and Chair of the Mosque and Community Affairs Committee of the Muslim Council of Britain, said that it gave him "tremendous pleasure" to see the growing number of young Muslim women adopting this practice as a "conscious choice." According to him, veiling was definitely seen by these women as a means of defending their Muslim identity in response to their minority status and the associated perceived sense of discrimination:

> Anyone in a minority status feels the need to keep their heritage alive as opposed to those in the majority who do not feel threatened or challenged.[45]

This reference to one's 'heritage' seems to be contradicted by the fact many of the forms of dress adopted often have little connection with one's culture or region of origin. Mogra believed that such practices were also an effort to assert their identity defining this on religious terms rather than ethnic: "Young people are much more educated and aware of their religion than their parents."

When asked why women – rather than young men – don't choose to wear their traditional form of dress (such as *shalwar kameez*) instead of a *hijab*, he said that it was to some extent due to preference for solidarity with a 'Muslim' identity rather than an ethnic minority identity, "especially since this [young] generation does not have any sense of back home in the way that their parents or grandparents do." Mogra explained that Muslims born in Britain do not have any memory or a strong, clear affinity with their parent's country of origin and they are increasingly negotiating their identity on the basis of their religion rather than 'ethnicity', especially when juxtaposed against the white majority (I. Mogra, personal communication, 17 August 2006).

While the specificities of young British Muslims, highlighted here by Mogra, ought to be taken into account, one also needs to acknowledge that this trend affects not only the UK but most Muslim countries and diaspora communities as well. It has been argued that this is a result of ongoing and sustained efforts by politically motivated forces to promote an international set of so-called 'Muslim uniforms'. WLUML in particular has pointed at 'the crucial role' played by "the religious right in identity politics everywhere, and the links that exist amongst politico-religious groups and between them" – as well as the fact that "definitions of collective identities [are] increasingly being hinged on definitions of gender so that the construction of a 'Muslim woman' is therefore integral to the construction of 'Muslimness'."[46]

However, not all imams in Britain advocate veiling for Muslim women. Dr. Mohammed Fahim, Chairman and Head Imam at the mosque and Muslim Community Centre in South Woodford (North-East London) believes that the recent surge in veiling practices is a "trivial matter" and that "what is more important is what is in the heart and soul." Responding to a comment by a British Pakistani man in his late twenties about his desire to find a good, *deeni* ('religious') wife who wears a *hijab*, Dr. Fahim tried to correct that man's perception of dress codes and what is or is not an Islamic requirement. Dr. Fahim explained to him that "there is a debate among Muslim scholars on the notion of *hijab* and dress codes for women… there are various interpretations and schools of thought and nothing is confirmed."[47]

Dr. Fahim was disappointed that "today, the headscarf has become a symbol – like a fashion." He traced the popularity of the garment to the 1973 Oil Crisis and the subsequent spread of the *Wahhabi* ideology (refer to the glossary for definition) in the Muslim world. He strongly believes that covering the head is not a religious obligation. "If people get angry when I say this, I say yes, Islam tells women to cover their breasts not the head."

He said that *burqas* and *jilbabs* were not compatible with British society and women here should not put themselves at a disadvantage by their dress and appearance and as a consequence lose out on job opportunities. Defending his rationale, he explained that at the time of the Prophet (PBUH), both men and women – Muslim and non-Muslim – covered their heads because of the hot, Arabian Desert sun. It was only after some 23 years since the first revelation that (as said in Surah Noor – of the

Qur'an), there was a message asking the believing women to "drop what you have on your head to your breasts." Dr. Fahim thinks that the reason for this revelation was to protect women's modesty, for men are attracted to a woman's body, not her hair. He therefore believes the emphasis is on covering women's breasts rather than the head. At the same time, he pointed out, the Qur'an asked the believing men to lower their gaze. (Dr. Fahim, personal communication, 2 June 2008)

Dr. Fahim also lamented British Muslim mothers' increasing desire to shroud their young, pre-pubescent daughters in *khimars* (refer to the glossary). He complained: "Why are these mothers depriving their little girls of their childhood?" He said the priority should instead be to teach children about modesty and education, ethics, manners, hospitality and mutual obligations to one another. (Dr. Fahim, personal communication, 2 June 2008)

While he was disappointed with the growing number of visible dress codes practiced among Muslim women in Britain, Dr. Fahim drew parallels with the proliferation of veiling in Egypt. He pointed out:

> Thirty years ago, you would never see anyone in Cairo dressed in a *khima*r or *hijab* – whatever you want to call it. My mother and my sisters were all very active, working women. They dressed very much like what you are wearing [referring to the author's full length trousers, shirt and full-sleeve jacket.] They were modest like that. But today when you walk down the streets of Cairo, you will see many, many young women with headscarves. (Dr. Fahim, personal communication, 2 June 2008)

This difference in perspective from two imams in many ways reflects the diversity of opinion within the Muslim community itself. While Mr. Ibrahim Mogra, a British-born and trained imam, was very sensitive to the security of a new (religious) identity provided by the veil to second and third-generation British Muslim women, Dr. Mohammad Fahim, a first generation Egyptian immigrant to the UK was less sympathetic to the veil's appeal.

4.4 Women's Experiences of Veiling

As mentioned earlier, all the 40 respondents who participated in this research belonged to the middle and upper socio-economic classes. All respondents wore only the *hijab* and had started doing so as a conscious choice while at university or later. When asked why they decided to veil, the immediate response was usually that it was a religious requirement. This was often followed by descriptions of how the practice benefited them and their understanding of why it was prescribed in the religion.

According to Fatima Syed, a twenty-four year old married woman from East London,

> The *hijab* makes me feel very confident. It is important for women's respect because we should not be taken as sexual objects. Wearing the *hijab* draws attention away from my physical appearance and allows people to rather focus on my spirituality and treat me as a person. (F. Syed, personal communication, 21 August 2006)

Fashionably dressed Hina Najeeb who works as an investment banker said:

> People say *hijab* is oppressive but I don't think so. Isn't it more oppressive to constantly try to meet set standards of beauty and an ideal which is propagated by advertisements of perfectly figured women with perfect faces? The *hijab* relieves us of these pressures and makes you focus on the real thing: inner beauty. (H. Najeeb, personal communication, 24 August 2006)

Some respondents cited key events in their lives as precipitating factors towards their decision to adopt the *hijab*. Sadia Bajwa explained that she was extremely 'inspired' by the *tafseer* lessons conducted in her neighbourhood by an Indian Muslim woman and decided to adopt the *hijab* after her first *hajj* (refer to the glossary for definition).

None of the mothers of the respondents in this survey adhered to similar modes of dress and the respondents did not claim to have received any encouragement from their parents in their decision to veil. Mothers of 60% of the respondents were working women and educated at least to secondary level. They reported wearing 'English clothes' at work and often relaxed in *shalwar kameez* at home and when socialising within the community. Of the 40% who did not work, none wore the *hijab* or *burqa*. Some did cover their heads with a *dupatta* but not as a matter of routine.

The veil evoked mixed reactions from respondents' families, friends and colleagues. Their parents were concerned about their safety in public given the increasing threat of Islamophobia in the country. In two cases, fathers appeared to be very worried about the impact of this on their daughters' prospects of finding a suitable (British) Pakistani spouse. Azmat Ali, himself a prominent figure in the local Muslim community of the London borough of Harrow (and member of the Council's Interfaith Committee as well as the Harrow Central Mosque's Committee), explained his concern about his daughter, Rohina Daud's 'sudden' decision to wear the *hijab* in 2005 as follows:

> They [young people] have so much distrust of this western society. Women, for example, my own daughter wears the *hijab*. Me and my wife are against it because look, if she is wearing the *hijab* she may not get married – because lots of people may not like the *hijab*. She is restricting herself. Professional people like doctors and educators want to socialise and be able to take their wives proudly around in their social circle. But if you wear the *hijab*, you know, you can't be accepted everywhere. (A. Ali, personal communication, 5 September 2006)

Resistance was also faced from mothers. The mother of twenty-six year old nutritionist, Saira Malik, was dismissive of her daughter's *hijab*:

> I don't like *hijab* – I don't like the whole thing and I would never like it for myself! I don't think it is necessary. (S. Malik, personal communication, 23 August 2006)

For these respondents of fairly liberal backgrounds, the *hijab* was not a tool to challenge parental or community control over their mobility as none had faced any opposition to their plans for higher education, employment, etc. They had grown up in relatively mixed and privileged neighbourhoods of London. Why then did these particular women decide to remain veiled in the face of such reactions?

Answers to these questions can be inferred from discussions about other aspects of their lives and their experiences of growing up as a Muslim minority in a Western country. These discussions clearly revealed that their inclination towards religion was a coping strategy designed to deal with their sense of isolation from the majority culture and a conscious assertion of identity:

> [After starting to wear the *hijab*] now when I step out on to the street, people perceive me as a Muslim. Other Muslims say salaam to me and recognise me as a Muslim. I really like that – I like to be recognised as a Muslim. (N. Khan, personal communication, 23 August 2006)

While most of the women interviewed had at least a couple of white, non-Muslim (and non South-Asian) British friends, they nonetheless were not permitted by their families to go to pubs and clubs as they were growing up. Even when they were allowed to join their English friends at the pub, the fact that they didn't consume any alcohol "automatically meant that we couldn't stay there for very long... When everyone is getting drunk around you, how long can you drink your orange juice and socialise?" said twenty-six year old Anila Khan from Watford. Anila Khan, a youth worker who works in a community centre in Watford with Muslim adolescents and teenagers with behavioural problems, was born in London to Pakistani parents from Mirpur, Kashmir. Khan started wearing the *hijab* in 2007 during the month of Ramadan. Dressed smartly in blue jeans, a colourful trendy white and purple shirt almost reaching her knees and a light blue scarf around her head, Khan met me at The Central Mosque of Brent, in Willesden Green (North London) as a fellow participant in a life coaching workshop in April 2008. Khan's mother is a housewife, educated up to class 10 (equivalent to GCSE) in her village in Mirpur while her father (of a similar educational level) owns a small family business. Khan said that a year ago, she would not even cover her hair with a *dupatta*, in spite of her mother's persistence, while visiting relatives in the city. She used to find it restrictive and unnecessary. She was always 'put off' by the "little group of *hijabis* at uni[versity] who always stuck together and never said salaam to you if you weren't a *hijabi* like them." But when her best friend started wearing the *hijab*, Khan felt her attitude change. "I went with her to some of her *tafseer* classes and met a lot of girls our age who were veiled, but they were not like the *hijabis* I knew at uni[versity]. These girls were normal, they had lives; they worked and did everything and yet also followed their religion."

When asked how she feels about her *hijab* or what changed after she started wearing it, she replied,

> The day I wore the *hijab*, it was like Allah placed a seed in my heart. It was the right time for me. Now I love it, I don't want to take it off. It is part of who I am. It hasn't changed anything else... except maybe that I have become more regular in my prayers, I have become more confident in who I am. (A. Khan, personal communication, 26 April 2008)

In a focus group discussion in May 2008 in London with five women, there was unanimous consensus that wearing the *hijab* was becoming increasingly difficult in Britain. Moneeba Ahmed, a twenty-four year old massage therapist and a martial arts student clad in a black headscarf and full-length *jilbab* from Plaistow (East London) reported:

> In this country, it is becoming difficult to cover. But *sabr* ('patience') is to remain steadfast and still cover. (M. Ahmed, personal communication, 18 April 2008)

Other participants agreed with this and shared their own experiences of street abuse:

> That sort of thing happens all the time. When you're walking to the corner off-licence, some man would just come up to you and call you all sorts of things just because you're wearing a *hijab*. They don't understand. And it's not just the men. The other day I was on the tube when this lady just kept staring at me and then said 'How do you breathe under that?' Once, when I was walking home alone at night, I was literally spat at. I guess you just have to remember, don't you, that you are doing it for yourself and for Allah. That love will give you the strength to bear this. (R. Siddiqui, personal communication, 18 April 2008)

Twenty-eight year old Aliya Kabir from Hounslow suggested that the best way to deal with such abuse is:

> Not to react; we shouldn't get distracted. For example, if your colleague derides you for praying during working hours, you just have to be tranquil. Be confident in who you are. (A. Kabir, personal communication, 18 April 2008)

In many ways, these women grew up in a parallel set-up and as one respondent described, found ways of having '*Halal* fun'. So instead of pubs and clubs, many young British Muslim women found a good alternative in the *sheesha* cafes of Edgware Road. These distinctions were apparent in some other areas of their lives as well such as earlier curfews during teenage years and restrictions on friendship with boys. These women grew up imbibing these values and now accept them as key Muslim values themselves and are keen to preserve them against what they see as a 'free society'.

The importance of clothing as an identity marker and a means of symbolic communication, where it gives Muslim women access and legitimacy to challenge traditional gender roles dictated by their community, or how it is perceived by wider society remains an important subject for contemporary Britain. Perhaps we are witnessing here the construction of a new British Muslim identity which is based on religion or religiosity for lack of other alternatives. There is no doubt that this tendency towards a homogenous Muslim identity superseding broader allegiances is a product of the type of state multiculturalism which has provided fertile ground for this identity construction to take root. The type of multiculturalism promoted in Britain has resulted in festering resentment and mistrust between faith groups, enabling them to become segregated from each other. This negative tolerance is a far cry from happy co-existence. In the name of diversity, this has in fact led to the loss of broader, progressive alliances of the past. Nonetheless, the situation in Britain is not all negative. Before we hasten to condemn multiculturalism altogether, we should remind ourselves of the state of integration and minority rights facing Muslim populations in countries such as France and Germany which do not follow a policy of multiculturalism. This comparative analysis is provided in Chapter 7 of this book.

Despite the British government's insistence on clustering together supposedly homogenous communities – with little attention paid to their internal power struggles and their position on women's rights – it seems that the younger Muslim women interviewed for this research have managed to carve out a distinctive voice for themselves. Whether they endorse or reject traditional gender roles, they are speaking out. Their assertion can be considered an expression of their agency – a posture which is directly juxtaposed to the stereotype of the veiled woman as a submissive recipient of propaganda and/or a victim of patriarchy.

Chapter 5: Faith-Based Schools

A considerable amount of research time was devoted to studying the educational system of England which includes many faith-based schools. In 2008, there were over 140 full-time Muslim schools in England[48] of which only five are state run[49]. The vast majority of these Muslim schools enforce a particular dress code for girls, starting from the uniform requirement of a headscarf. This chapter examines the debate surrounding Muslim faith-schools in Britain, their role in promoting specific dress codes and how this impacts the gender ideology of the community.

According to a 2006 survey conducted for the Channel 4 television documentary series, 'Dispatches', half of the one thousand Muslims interviewed across the UK favoured Muslim faith schools as a preferred option for their children. In the UK, 'faith schools' refers to any school with a religious character. The term is used to refer to full-time day or boarding schools which follow the national curriculum, but include extra provision for religious instruction. In this way, they differ from other state (funded) or private schools which are supposed to provide a secular learning environment for children. There is a wide range of faith schools catering to the needs of different faith communities in Britain: Church of England, Muslim, Catholic, Jewish and Sikh. These may or may not benefit from state funding. Only five of the 140 Muslim schools are fully supported by state funding.

While faith schools are required to follow the national curriculum, they are not obligated by law to formally teach Religious Education (RE) to their students at any level[50]. Muslim faith schools' admission policy is determined by their governing authorities and while most offer admission to non-Muslim pupils, they can legally restrict it to Muslims only.

The British Government's Education Bill 2002 encourages religious organisations to submit proposals to meet any identified need for new schools. As such, faith schools form an essential strategy of the Government's education reforms intended to increase parental choice while encouraging religious education. This was clearly Blair's policy, and linked to the multiculturalist policies discussed earlier.

The Government's policy is that faith schools should be retained as a good alternative for those seeking to educate their children in a faith-based environment, citing better academic performance/results to support its view. It also believes that these schools encourage those families to send their children to school that would not be comfortable sending them to regular schools. In an effort to strengthen the capacity of these schools, the Department for Education and Skills is trying to make it easier for independent faith schools, particularly Muslim ones, to opt into the state sector and access state funds. It has already allocated £100,000 to the Association of Muslim Schools to assist 120 independent Muslim schools access these funds as 'voluntary-aided' schools. This measure to include Muslim schools into the state sector is supported by the Conservative Party as well (in opposition at time of going to print).

From the State's perspective, offering financial assistance may be a way to gain some control over the curriculum and educational culture in these Muslim faith schools. It is possibly seen as a regulatory measure to minimise the possibility of import of transnational Islamic fundamentalist ideologies from abroad.

While Muslim community leaders and institutions understandably welcomed this move (in 2005) almost two-thirds of the public opposed these plans to increase the number of state-funded faith schools as they view it as a barrier to social cohesion[51]. Newspaper articles as well as statements by key government officials have raised concerns about the impact of Muslim schools on integration with many fearing that these may lead to greater segregation of communities. Chairman of the Commons Education Select Committee, Barry Sheerman's September 2005 statement reflects this perspective:

> Do we want a ghettoised education system? Schools play a crucial role in integrating different communities and the growth of faith schools poses a real threat to this. These things need to be thought through very carefully before they are implemented.

David Bell, the chief inspector of schools, joined in with criticism of Muslim schools saying they posed a challenge to the coherence of British society. In a speech to the Hansard society, Mr Bell said that "traditional Islamic education does not entirely prepare pupils for their lives as Muslims in modern Britain."[52] It is noteworthy that this debate has focused exclusively on Muslim faith schools and not on other denominational schools, such as Jewish or Sikh ones.

Critics of faith schools who believe that they lead to more segregated communities include members of certain Muslim women's civil society organisations and academics as well. They fear that the government is playing into the hands of fundamentalist[53] forces (from among the community as well as certain institutions) by appeasing their demands for separate schools. They view this as a very dangerous trend for it directly stands to bolster these fundamentalist forces' attempt to stifle dissent and exert absolute control over the lives of Muslims – women specifically. They disagree with the vision of community, which these forces seek to create through such schools. Among other things, they see it as an institutionalised regulation of British Muslim girls' lives to check that they conform to an expected standard of modesty and morality often according to a singular, rigid interpretation of Islam. For instance, where the uniform policy entails a *hijab* or *shalwar kameez* for girls, a school could be seen to define a certain dress code as an ideal for its Muslim, female students.

Nevertheless, Muslim schools enjoy widespread support among the community as many would rather to enrol their children there if they are satisfied with the quality of education offered. While there is no available means to assert this statistically it was evident from the opinions expressed by half of the respondents consulted for this research. Their principal objective in sending their daughters to single sex schools was to protect them from 'unnecessary distractions'. However, the determinating factor for their choice of school was the quality of education and the reputation of the school, and most suspected that Muslim schools in Britain were not yet on a par with mainstream schools. This lack of trust in the current capacity of Islamic schools was reflected in the decision of Hafiz Akram, Harrow Central Mosque's Imam to send his own sixteen year old daughter to the local all-girls state school (Bentley Wood High School) rather than a Muslim school. So while the respondents seemed supportive of the idea of Muslim schools and hoped that they would develop into hubs of quality education, they were reluctant to admit their (future) daughters to these schools as they did not think that the current level of the schools matched the quality offered elsewhere[54].

None of them opposed the growth of Muslim schools and some held a certain degree of respect for them. In fact, most participants viewed this growth as a positive development. The appeal of Muslim schools to the community lies not just in their role providing a Muslim education and a favourable social environment to Muslim students, but also as a shield against racism. In an ethnographic study conducted by Saeeda Khanum at the Muslim Girls' School in Bradford, students described what they liked about the school:

> We get to learn all about our religion and can pray when we like. There is no racism here. No one here laughs at the way we dress, because we are all the same.[55]

It was interesting to note that the vast majority of those interviewed (mainly women) who support single-sex education for their children had themselves attended mixed state or private schools. This demonstrates the growing importance attached to (so-called) 'Muslim' values and traditions among second and third generation British Muslims compared to the first wave of immigrants to Britain.

The evidence indicates that the growth of Muslim schools holds more significance for the community than simply its functional utility in offering an Islamic education. It also represents the expansion of public space captured by British Muslims – it is a vehicle for their assertion of minority rights and religious identity. To a great degree, it is an extension of the education movement which began in the 1970s and 1980s with demands for *halal* meals and separate changing rooms for boys and girls in state schools. This evolution then prompts the question of whether this is a successful strategy for the community, particularly for its women members. Given that much of the student body is Muslim, does a faith school allow the next generation of British Muslim citizens sufficient opportunity for integration into British society? Or, as many fear, are these schools, with their emphasis on Islam and a specific form of Muslim identity, creating a parallel (and separate) community?

In prescribing a 'modest' dress code for women, staff and girls, represented by the *hijab*, are these schools inadvertently reinforcing the trend towards a homogenous, singular British Muslim identity?

Only three of the 40 respondents interviewed in this project had attended Muslim schools. When asked about their experiences, two of them explained that the main difference between a regular (secular) school and a Muslim school is that the teachers were mainly or exclusively women, the uniform policy followed 'Islamic principles' of modesty and that the student body was segregated by sex. Both these participants went on to pursue higher education. One of them reported that she only wore the *hijab* in school as part of the uniform, but took it off after school hours.

The experience of the third research participant who attended a Muslim school in London provides another lengthier perspective about the impact of faith schools on the 'gender roles' advocated by the community. Twenty-five year old Aisha Dodwell from London was born to English converts to Islam. She attended a Muslim faith school for most of her primary education but then moved on to three different state secondary schools (including a non-denominational school, a Catholic and a Church of England school.) Much of the remaining section of this chapter is devoted to her personal account of Muslim schooling, reflecting as it does a comprehensive comparison with secular schooling.

Aisha recalled her experience of studying at a high-profile Muslim school:

> As my mother was a teacher at the school, I was not only a pupil but was greatly involved in the wider school community. As I am now 25, I will attempt to recall my experiences and feeling in order to reflect upon how being a girl in a Muslim school can have long term impacts upon gender in society.
>
> The school was very conservative and built into the standard national curriculum were a large amount of religious classes, Qur'an lessons, Arabic classes and we all attended regular prayer sessions. The girls were all required to wear headscarves as part of the uniform, and I recall this being enforced rather strictly. I can remember on a few occasions being disciplined for having my hair slipping out from the front of my headscarf.
>
> Girls were encouraged to be educated as much as the boys by all means, and the overall level of education was very high. Issues affecting gender roles were what would be expected from a conservative Muslim school, headscarves, women sitting behind boys in prayers and boys being allowed to go to the local Mosque for Friday prayers… Everything I was taught at home about rights and wrongs and what it meant to be a girl was reinforced at my school, so it all felt very normal to me as a child.
>
> The first school I attended after leaving the Muslim school was a mixed non-denominational school where I can remember being extremely confused by many of the things they did such as mixed dance classes or getting changed together for PE. Going to a different school and realising that not everybody lived as we did had a big influence on my life. I think in the long term simply being surrounded by diverse people and developing non-Muslim friendships did enable me to reflect critically on the religion and religious rules. If I had stayed in Islamic school throughout my education and only had Muslim friends, I possibly would not have had the space to critically view what I was being taught. I see that there were both negatives and positives to attending Muslim faith school.

In general, I feel that the role of [the] faith school and requirement to wear a headscarf as part of the uniform does not have either an obvious, direct or homogenous effect on women in the long term. I know of friends who stayed in Muslim school for their whole education and who then went on to British universities and now, in their adult lives, do not wear headscarves and have occupations that may not be considered by some Muslims as particularly appropriate (band promoter/artist). While at the same time, I also know of many Muslim girls who went to non-denominational schools where they were not forced to wear headscarves by the school, but as adults they still wear headscarves and follow a more strict line of Islam.

From my personal experiences, I feel that if attending a Muslim school and having a headscarf in the uniform had any long lasting effects on me personally they were probably only subconscious ones. As a child I enjoyed wearing a headscarf and did not see it as a negative thing at all. But when reflecting on this part of my childhood, perhaps that by being consistently told that I had to dress 'modestly' and being taught that girls who did not cover up, and who dressed more 'immodestly' were bad people, did create a definite schism with non-Muslims. I was always under the impression that women who wore shorts and vest tops for example, were bad/loose women who did not know the true way. These ideas were deeply ingrained in me as a child, and I remember feeling particularly confused as my cousins, who were non-Muslim, seemed like nice people despite dressing so 'immodestly'. (A. Dodwell, personal communication, 29 January 2009.)

Reflecting on the uniform policy, Dodwell linked the headscarf requirement to community solidarity and identity formation. Her testimony also highlights the role of dress code in introducing – both physically and visually – a separation which defines who belongs to the community and who does not. As highlighted by Yuval-Davis and Sahgal[56], community members, if they behave according to rules, can enjoy a deep sense of security.

I feel that this uniform, particularly the headscarf was a way in which we were taught to identify ourselves, and in identifying who we were as Muslim kids in the UK, I think it was important for the community to teach us who was not a part of 'us'. One of the most vivid feelings I have from the school was the feeling of belonging to a community that was different from everyone else around us. We were taught that everyone else had it all wrong (which of course is intrinsic to any religion) but this was really reinforced by physically creating a difference through the headscarf. I suppose the headscarf was an important part of forming this identity. As a child I think I felt reassured to be part of such a secure community, though was always unsure that everyone else could really be so wrong. I also remember that people were very curious about us, and we would often have television cameras in the school playground for some documentary or other. I can also recall people often looking in through the playground fence; perhaps in the '80s it was more curious to see a school full of girls wearing headscarves.

This uniform prescription apparently also curtailed girls' participation in sports in the school – a fact that is often justified with reference to modesty but also carries unfounded fears related to virginity (girls practising sports are said to be at risk of rupturing their hymen). So crucial are these concerns – at least for girls – that physical activity is seen as potentially challenging the very essence of prescribed gender roles. If one 'indulges', it must therefore remain a 'secret': as noted earlier, the security and support afforded by the community require compliance, or at least avoiding any open challenge of the accepted rules:

> Enforcing strict dress codes for girls and women also impacts heavily with regard to activities and sports. From my personal experience I particularly remember having a problem with swimming. Once I reached puberty it was totally out of the question that I would be allowed to go swimming due to the nature of the costume. Muslim women that I know who do go swimming go to women's only sessions and wear costumes that cover their whole bodies which again only reinforces schisms with non-Muslims. When I was at Muslim school, my mother allowed me to go to dance classes outside of school once a week. I remember having to keep this secret from everyone at the school as I understood that wearing a leotard would have been totally unacceptable, and some would have had a problem with the nature of dance itself. When I left the Muslim school, I was allowed to do things that would have never been allowed in a Muslim school: attend scouts where we did out-door activities, and I was able to be open about attending dance classes. Being allowed to do these activities was clearly a benefit of being out of the strong holds of faith school, which clearly meant that a wider range of activities became open to me. (A. Dodwell, personal communication, 29 January 2009)

Responding to the question of the long-term impact of Muslim faith-schools on the gender ideology of the community, Dodwell did not think that enforcing a religious dress code in school had any impact of her educational achievement:

> In terms of gender roles, looking back on my life as a Muslim girl – the only girl in the family – I can see that I had very different expectations put upon me in comparison with my brothers. I think of the subtle things such as wearing a headscarf and having to battle with what I was allowed to wear while my brothers could wear what they wanted…. Although we did have positive female role-models as most of the teachers were women, these reinforced typical gender roles in that the teachers were mostly women, while all the positions of authority, such as the Imams and head-teacher were all men. I think that going to the school only reinforced what I was getting from home, that men were the ultimate authority figures. Of course, my brothers were encouraged to achieve academically, while my education was not seen as particularly important, my father always told me it was more important that I be happy in order to be a good mother or wife. For certain this upbringing has impacts upon my life now, and I'm sure women with similar upbringings have found the same. However, the reality is that I have in fact achieved far more academically than any of my brothers. Thus having religious dress codes enforced on a child probably does not have negative effects on the individual's educational achievements. (A. Dodwell, personal communication, 29 January 2009)

Dodwell's assessment is that the negative repercussion of Muslim schooling alone (notwithstanding the other influences already existing within the community) is most important on integration and social cohesion:

> I don't know that a Muslim faith school in itself can impact upon women as the school only reinforces what the religion teaches. It is difficult to distinguish the influences from school and from outside school. Wearing the headscarf and all other expectations of girls that were applied by the school were only what was being encouraged by the religion more generally. I would imagine that a lot of Muslim girls who go to mixed faith schools probably have the same expectations from home, and likely attend Mosque school on the weekend anyway. However, I do think that where faith schools probably had a more clear effect was in encouraging and maintaining a schism between Muslims and non-Muslims. (A. Dodwell, personal communication, 29 January 2009)

This denotes the impact of faith schools on women as it reinforces the gender roles propagated by the community. This is the most important aspect to note about the impact of faith schools and one which is much more important than the quality of education offered. If faith schools, through admission policies, curriculum, gender segregated seating plans and uniforms provide a atmosphere wholly different from the mainstream, do they adequately prepare their students (both male and female) to integrate and engage with the rest of British society upon graduation?

Dodwell's experience was juxtaposed to two other respondents of this research who reported very positive experiences of attending faith schools in London. Twenty-two year old Sarah Amjad, attended the Islamia Girls School in Harrow (North West London) where the *hijab* was part of the uniform. The girls-only school had a strict policy of recruiting only female teachers for its pupils. Sarah Amjad, who grew up wearing the *hijab*, graduated from the School in 2004 and is now studying medicine at University College London. A confident and cheerful young woman, she takes part in community activities and volunteers at a Muslim community centre in North London.

Similarly, Ayesha Zahra, a twenty-one year old student of English Literature at Queen Mary, University of London, attended an Islamic school which had separate campuses for boys and girls. With the exception of art, no classes were held in a co-education environment. Zahra cited a very positive experience of her school years; she said that because the *hijab* was part of the uniform, everyone who attended the school accepted this requirement. However, she pointed out that there were many 'non-*hijabis*' in the classroom as well who only wore the *hijab* in school and took it off when they went home. (A. Zahra, personal communication, 18 May 2008)

The debate over the right of parents to choose between a faith school and state non-denominational school is not only a question of policy between the Muslim community and the UK education authorities but also a major issue within the Muslim community itself. On the one hand, there is little doubt that Muslim minorities, particularly those of Asian origin, experience considerable discrimination in society. The faith-based school may, as many proponents of Muslim schooling argue, provide a safe space for young students to flourish and feel confident in their identity. On the other hand, this protective environment which is conducive to their personal development and learning, may be impeding young British Muslim graduates of these schools from living comfortably as integrated members of British society. For girls, the extent to which this protective environment is beneficial is a different question. They may be shielded from racism and Islamophobia, but is this replaced by a greater vulnerability to sexism (justified in the name of religion)?

Girls are discouraged to practice sports and dance. They are reprimanded if their hair shows under the *hijab*. They are told their academic achievements are less important than motherhood and marriage. The fact that the 3 interviewees overcome this, or are able to take advantage of (traditional yet) positive female role models, is a testimony to the fact that women struggle to assert themselves, rather than the 'protective environment' being conducive to girls' achievements.

The few interviews conducted for this research do not suggest that Muslim schools are promoting practices and beliefs which compromise women's rights and curtail their options (on a normative level) anymore than other influences in the community. The schools' impact on the gender ideology of the community is mostly to reinforce these influences. The uniform requirement of the headscarf is a means of teaching Muslim girls to identify themselves as Muslim in the UK, and this piece of cloth then plays an important role in distinguishing their identity as visibly distinct from the rest of British society. While the restrictions girls face at school do not necessarily have a more negative impact upon them than the gender discrimination they face at home or in the community, the type of religious instruction on offer legitimises these barriers as a divine order. It is this point which is of utmost significance in the discourse on Muslim faith-schools as it can widen the schism between Muslims and non-Muslims and touches at the very core of the debate on integration, multiculturalism and women's rights.

Unfortunately, the respondent sample in this research project is too limited to render a definitive conclusion on the impact of faith schools. For this purpose, future research on the subject should adopt a methodology which effectively examines the role of women in the leadership and management of Muslim schools, the participation of Muslim women in the Board of Governors of Muslim schools and the role models set by the school teachers.

Chapter 6: Veiling and Empowerment Strategies

The UK is a country where veiling and publicly embracing religiosity have been used by Muslim women to rid themselves of some of the cultural practices imposed on them in the name of Islam. Women are separating culture from religion in their struggles for empowerment, and the veil can be (and is for some women) an important vehicle in this process. Many are re-interpreting the Qur'an and are engaging in theological discussions to come up with a women-centred interpretation. This struggle stands out in their fierce assertion of identity in community media, their resistance to forced and early marriages and their increasing confidence to find Muslim husbands from outside their parents' communities of origin. In all these struggles women are relying on Islamic arguments (derived from religious texts) and the human rights framework to support their decisions rather than alluding to 'modernity'. In escaping rigid, traditional patriarchal norms while remaining within the framework of religion, they are increasingly able to expand the choices available to them and assert their rights in relation to key life issues while retaining the respect and support of the community.

Meanwhile, the wider non-Muslim society is often ignorant of these battles. In condemning the veil as a symbol of women's oppression, the wider British society is denying the agency of the women who have chosen to take up the veil and through which they are empowering themselves to break away at least from some of the oppressive cultural practices of their communities of origin. This chapter considers how some of these struggles manifest themselves, specifically in terms of access to education, the labour market and sports.

6.1 Demanding space for Veiling in British Schools

School uniforms have been a source of concern for some British Muslims since the early days of settlement of Muslim families in Britain in the 1960s. Over the years, British schools have allowed trousers and long, ankle-length skirts as alternative uniform options for their female pupils. Ahmed Versi, Editor of the *Muslim News* recalls:

> Until the '80s and '90s, many schools in the UK did not allow Muslim girls to wear headscarves, as that was considered to be not part of the school uniform. We repeatedly published cases of such human rights abuses in almost every issue, through features, interviews, comments and cartoons. Finally, the Tory (Conservative Party) Head of Education at that time

announced guidelines for the schools to take religious sensitivities, including dress code, into account when formulating school uniform policies.[57]

In Versi's analysis, the lack of any standardised legislation or directives from the Department for Education and Skills (DfES) guiding schools to be sensitive to the needs of their female Muslim students was the main reason for discontent (A. Versi, personal communication, 23 July 2008). The Department for Children, Schools and Families and the Department for Innovation, Universities and Skills, have now taken over the responsibilities of the DfES.

Dress codes issues are systematically raised with reference to female students and instructors, never male. This suggests that the concerns are less about religious sensitivity and particularities and more about gender roles and modesty. Inadvertently, this means that the onus of defending and representing the Muslim community once again falls on Muslim women.

Since 9/11, schools have become the platforms for some of the most hotly contested debates on the veil. However, while most schools allow headscarves to be worn as part of the school uniform, the debate has now evolved to focus more on whether the *jilbab* and *niqabs* can be worn on the school premises by students and teachers. The past few years have witnessed a number of legal cases involving Muslim girls seeking judicial recourse to observe various types of dress codes in school.

One particularly high-profile case involving a seventeen year old student, Shabina Begum of Denbigh High School in Luton (Bedfordshire), received a lot of media attention and stimulated public debate on the issue.

With a (79%) Muslim-majority student body, Denbigh High School allows Muslim pupils to wear *shalwar kameez* as an alternative uniform option. Shabina had followed this policy until 2002 when at the age of 15 she decided to wear the *jilbab* to school. She was asked to remove her *jilbab* and wear the approved uniform in class in order to continue attending the school. The school maintained that her new attire was not appropriate school uniform, arguing that the option of *shalwar kameez* already reflected its willingness to adequately meet the needs of its Muslim students and community. The school had offered this uniform option after consulting the Department of Education and Skills (DfES), pupils, parents, schools, leading Muslim organisations and Islamic scholars. The school cited that the country's largest mosque in London had confirmed that the *shalwar kameez* conformed to Islamic standards of modesty. It had reportedly rejected attempts at mediation or compromise on the issue when Shabina proposed wearing her *jilbab* in the school colours so as to be identified as a member of the school community.

However, Shabina, who was represented by the Children's Legal Centre[58], challenged Denbigh High School, its board of governors, and the Local Education Authority (LEA) for excluding her, and for violating her right to freedom of religion and her right to education. Her case was high-profile because the team of lawyers from the Children's Legal Centre, that defended her case, was led by Cherie Blair (wife of Tony Blair, the British Prime Minister from May 1997 to June 2007). By the time the matter went to court, she had already missed over a year of schooling. She had lost her first case at the High Court on 15 June 2004. Reactions to this judgment from the major Muslim institutions of the country reflected the diversity of opinion among the community itself. The Muslim Council of Britain found this decision to be a denial of Shabina's "right to wear the *jilbab* to school" as "worrying and objectionable."[59]

Dr. Ghayasuddin of the Muslim Parliament, on the other hand, welcomed the judgment saying that, "when making demands, Muslims have to remain within the limits of reason…[and] while asserting their cultural identity Muslims should avoid allowing themselves to be driven to extremes by expressions of Islamophobic sentiment."[60]

The Commission for Racial Equality had, however, in 2004, determined that the School's unwillingness to accommodate Shabina's request constituted 'indirect racism'.

Subsequently, Shabina appealed this High Court ruling. In what was widely hailed as a landmark ruling in March 2005, the Court of Appeals upheld Shabina's complaint stating that the school had interfered with her right to manifest her religion by refusing to allow her to wear a *jilbab* and thus violated the Human Rights Act. This ruling was based on the Children's Legal Centre's argument that the school's actions amounted to unlawful exclusion, and were a denial of the right to education under Article 2(1) of the European Convention on Human Rights (ECHR) and in breach of her right to religious freedom under Article 9(1) of the ECHR, and Section 6 of the Human Rights Act.[61]

This ruling was then welcomed by the MCB as a 'common-sense approach':

The British Muslim community is a diverse community in terms of the interpretation and understanding of their faith and its practice. Within this broad spectrum, those that believe and choose to wear the *jilbab* and consider it to be part of their faith requirement for modest attire should be respected. (Iqbal Sacranie, then MCB Secretary-General)[62]

The view of imams in Luton that the *shalwar kameez* fulfilled the requirements of 'Islamic' dressing was supported by Dr. Anas Abushadya, Imam of the London Central Mosque – one of the most important seats of Islam in the UK. But Imam Dr. Abduljalil Sajid, chairman of the Muslim Council for Religious and Racial Harmony, says for a strict Muslim, conforming to 'Islamic' guidelines may not be enough: "The shalwar kameez is modest dress no doubt, but it's Indian/Pakistani dress rather than Islamic."[63]

This is a poignant statement of what is defined as appropriate Muslim dress – is its 'authenticity' derived from Arab culture only? Many Muslims in Britain as well as Muslim-majority countries are increasingly worried about the 'Arabisation' of Muslim dress codes particularly as Arabs are only a minority of the Muslim population worldwide. Thus many Muslims are reluctant to espouse these dress codes which they consider to be rooted in Arab culture, but garbed as authentic 'Islamic' practice.

Shadow education secretary (of the Conservative Party), Tim Collins said it should be for 'schools alone' to decide their dress code. "This case yet again reflects the way in which the Human Rights Act is unduly restricting the freedom of head teachers to run their schools in their own way", he said.[64]

However, a year later, the 2005 Court of Appeal ruling was overturned by a unanimous ruling of the House of Lords judges on 22 March 2006.[65] According to the House of Lords, the School had "taken immense pains to devise a uniform policy which respected Muslim beliefs… (and had done so) in an inclusive, unthreatening and uncompetitive way."

They said: "The rules laid down were as far from being mindless as uniform rules could ever be…. It appeared the rules were acceptable to mainstream Muslim opinion." The House of Lords ruled that there was no interference with Shabina Begum's right to religious freedom as the School had already devised a policy which respected her religious beliefs and that it had a lawful right to uphold its policy.

Supporting this ruling, a DfES spokesman said, "What an individual pupil should or should not wear in school is a matter for individual schools in consultation with parents."[66]

Boris Johnson (elected the Mayor of London in 2008) was a Conservative Party MP for Henley in 2006 and wrote an article in support of the judgment in the right-wing newspaper, the Telegraph as follows:

> I don't know whether you caught young Shabina Begum talking on the television yesterday, but, as I studied the pictures of this exceedingly good-looking and confident young woman, I was suddenly conscious of a paradox.
>
> Here she is, at the centre of a national media storm, and one that has been very largely whipped up by her own supporters. There goes our Shabina, batting her (rather beautiful) eyes through her visor, and thereby exciting the interest of millions of otherwise apathetic viewers, who are not only infidels but very possibly male infidels at that.
>
> This is the seventeen year old from Luton whose dress sense and physical form are now the number one subject for conversation in every household in the country; and yet for years we have been asked to believe that the reason she wanted to vindicate her right to break school rules, and wear a [*tent*] instead of [*shalwar kameez*], was to protect – in the word of her lawyer, Cherie Blair – her 'modesty'. (Italics author's own for emphasis)[67]

Needless to say, the tone of his article was sexist and patronising. Boris Johnson continued defending the judgment with the following comment:

> All around us, in our courts, in the oppressive liberty-destroying Bills being rushed through Parliament, we see the disasters of multiculturalism, the system by which too many Muslims have been allowed to grow up in this country with no sense of loyalty to its institutions, and with a sense of complete apartness.
>
> In rejecting Shabina's case, the Law Lords have provided a small but important victory for good sense, for British cohesion, and for the right of teachers to run their own schools.

Shabina's own response to the judgment reflected her determination to contest the ruling and her perception of what is the proper, prescribed form of modest dress for women: "*Shalwar kameez* does not satisfy Islamic clothing.... I feel it is an obligation upon Muslim women to wear this [the *jilbab*] although there are many other opinions."[68]

A year earlier in 2005, when she won the Court of Appeals ruling, Shabina celebrated the occasion as:

> [A] victory for all Muslims who wish to preserve their identity and values. [...] As a young woman growing up in post-9/11, I have witnessed a great deal of bigotry and prejudice from the media, politicians and legal officials. This bigotry resulted from my choice to wear a piece of cloth, not as of force, but as of [*sic*] belief in Islam.

Speaking outside court, Shabina, who then moved on to another school where the *jilbab* was allowed, said Denbigh High School's action could not be viewed merely as a local decision taken in isolation.

> Rather it was a consequence of an atmosphere that has been created in western societies post 9/11, an atmosphere in which Islam has been made a target for vilification in the name of the 'War on Terror'. It is amazing that in the so-called free world I have to fight to wear this attire. This amazement has not been left unnoticed in my community. The Muslim community has seen a concerted effort to dehumanise Muslims and vilify Islam.... I hope that my case would give strength to others.[69]

She is presently at university and also presents the BBC Asian Network Report, 'Symbol-ed Out'.

Notwithstanding the sensationalistic reporting of her case, with journalists in the print media commenting on the style and colours of each and every item of her clothing, a closer look at the players involved in her case reveals the underlying political motivations of her supporters. Many news reports highlighted that her legal guardian, her brother, had links with the Islamist political party Hizb-ut-Tahrir (HT). In every newspaper and television interview that she gave, Shabina vehemently denied allegations of coercion: "No. People say my brother forced me, but my sister is not orthodox: how come she has not been 'forced'? I am an intelligent person: I know there are organisations that could help me if I were forced."[70]

In her confident articulation of her case in front of the cameras, she challenged the stereotype of 'passive Muslim women' that filled many of the media reports, insisting on her own agency.

However, it is clear that Shabina had been in contact with HT since 2004 – a fact that helps draw links between a seemingly individual case, which has polarized the UK national scene, and its connections with political Islam, locally as well as abroad. HT is a global Islamist political organisation which aims to re-establish the Islamic Caliphate as an independent state to unify the Muslim world (Muslim-majority countries). It was founded in 1953 by Taqiuddin an-Nabhani, a scholar, politician and judge in the Court of Appeals in Jerusalem. Today it operates throughout the world and has an office in London. The organisation has a considerable membership in the UK and actively recruits through outreach on British campuses. The party is banned in several countries, including Muslim countries. It is viewed with deep suspicion by sections of the British Muslim community as well as the state. In August 2005, former Prime Minister Tony Blair announced plans to ban the party but the Government retreated from this position two years later.

HT has women members but its stance on women's rights is far from progressive. It considers the primary role of a woman to be that of a wife and a mother. It believes that women's honour needs to be guarded and espouses a strict gender ideology which advocates the segregation of the sexes in the public sphere. On the issue of women's dress, it believes that women should cover their heads and bodies with an outer garment (except for their face and hands). Interestingly, the HT does recognise women's right to employment, right to vote (but not compete for ruling positions), right to inheritance and custody of children after divorce.

A member of the party, Dr Nazreen Nawaz, representative of women in Hizb ut-Tahrir's, confirmed she had advised Shabina:

> We offered her general support. She just needed encouragement. Our work in the West is about explaining Islam to the community. I first had contact with her about a year ago (i.e. spring 2004). It was to give general advice about the Islamic view on the issue of the *jilbab*. But it needs to be stressed she is somebody who thinks for herself. She has discovered Islam for herself.[71]

Shabina was orphaned in 2004 when her mother died from a brain haemorrhage (her father died when she was three) and she lives with her brother and an elder sister. While the family kept denying any manipulation of Shabina, Labour Party MPs and the media continued to be suspicious of her brother's alleged links with HT. The London newspaper, the Evening Standard quoted the local Labour MP for Luton South, Margaret Moran:

> The community's view was very, very strongly that this had nothing to do with the girl's education but that this was a political stunt made by a fundamentalist group. The word in the community is her brother is a member of Hizb ut-Tahrir. The imams know it, the community leaders know it. My view is this has been engineered by the brother and I feel very sad for this girl... this has nothing to do with education or uniforms.

Similarly, the paper quoted prominent Muslim politician Khalid Mahmood, Labour MP for Birmingham Perry Bar: "She [Shabina] has been used as a political football by Hizb ut-Tahrir. They have been working on this girl. They want an Islamic revolution and they will try to disrupt anybody they can." Indeed the level of articulation and choice of words used in some of the statements read by her outside court hearings indicate strong support from Islamist forces such as HT and highlight the role of her brother, as they seem to be above the level of expression of a teenager.

A similar case in Buckinghamshire, which resulted in a ruling upholding the school's right to ban the *niqab* in the classroom, prompted the DfES to finally issue clear guidance to schools on the issue of dress codes. The new guidance issued on 20 March 2007, calls for schools to continue forming their uniform policy in consultation with the community, but allows them to ban pupils from wearing full-face veils on security, safety or learning grounds. The guidance, stressed that teachers in the classroom needed to be able to identify individual pupils in order to maintain discipline and judge their engagement with learning, or secure their participation in discussions and practical activities.

Schools minister Jim Knight insisted on interaction with the local community, but reaffirmed the schools' prerogative to define their own policy with regards to dress codes:

> Schools should consult parents and the wider community when setting uniform policy. And while they should make every effort to accommodate social, religious or medical requirements of individual pupils, the needs

of safety, security and effective learning in the school must always take precedence.[72]

On 7 May 2007, the Lord Chancellor, Lord Falconer, the Government's legal chief, ruled that the *niqab* can be ruled out on the grounds of school uniform policy. He confirmed that the ruling included other Islamic religious garments such as the full-length *jilbab*. While declaring this to a conference of the National Association of Head Teachers, he added that he expressed his support for the decision of the Denbigh High School head teacher in the Shabina Begum case:

> The case showed how uniform can be a difficult issue and one where head teachers and the school's governing body have to think extremely carefully. But more than that, it showed that common sense and human rights are entirely in line each other.[73]

This much-awaited uniform guidance from the DfES was welcomed by many sections (though not all) of the Muslim community, as well as by teachers, who had for years complained about the lack of a coherent national policy/best practice guidelines regarding religious dress in educational institutions. Prior to issuing the 2007 guidance, the DfES had maintained that the rules on dress codes and symbols were not its responsibility, but that of the governors of each school. This caused some confusion especially given that the wearing of the *kippa* and *turban* was protected by the Race Relations Act 1976 under which Jews and Sikhs are considered racial groups. Muslims do not benefit from the Act in the same way as they are not considered a race and cannot have their interests protected in this respect. This discrepancy resulted in sporadic cases brought by Muslim girls trying to observe so-called 'Islamic' forms of dress codes against schools that were unwilling to accommodate their demand. These schools usually argued from the standpoint that these pupils disrupted school discipline and learning opportunities. However, it must be noted that these cases have emerged in the past five years (mostly since 2003-2004) and were not reported on such a scale earlier.

These cases also underline attitudes in wider society: while workplaces and educational institutions have learnt to accommodate the headscarf, the full-face veil or the *niqab* provokes strong opposition. Historically, the *niqab* has not been considered a requirement for observant Muslim women and in fact that there are scholars in Egypt who believe that it is a Middle Eastern customary practice rather than one derived from Islam.

In late 2006, the debate shifted from Muslim students to teachers as the suspension of a twenty-three year old teaching assistant, Aishah Azmi, from the state-funded Church of England, Voluntary Controlled Headfield junior school, run by the Kirklees Council (in Dewsbury) for refusal to remove her face-veil in the classroom captured media attention. Azmi, a teaching assistant focused on developing primary school children's linguistic skills, particularly those pupils who were bi-lingual. At the time of her recruitment, Azmi only wore the *hijab*. When she started her employment she requested that she be allowed to wear the *niqab* and the school initially agreed. However, the school soon requested her to remove her face veil when teaching the children in the classroom as it impeded communication. The school's standpoint was that children needed to be able to visually see the movement of Azmi's lips in order to learn the proper pronunciation of words. However, Azmi responded that she would only remove the veil if no male member of staff was present. This stipulation was deemed unacceptable by her employer, Kirklees Council, who suspended her (she remained on full salary) pending the outcome of the tribunal case.

Azmi protested her suspension at an employment tribunal claiming that she had been discriminated against on religious grounds and that she had been victimised as a result of her complaints. The tribunal dismissed three claims of religious discrimination and harassment, but awarded her £1,000 in compensation for hurt feelings. Furthermore, because in dealing with her grievance the school had not followed minimum grievance procedures set out in the law, it was bound to increase this award by between 10% and 50%. It chose the minimum increase of 10% and therefore awarded her £1,100 in total. At the same time, the tribunal rebuked ministers for intervening in the case by giving public statements in support of the school's action against Azmi. Azmi was subsequently dismissed by Kirklees Council.

This verdict was widely supported by Muslim and non-Muslim politicians alike. During the course of the case, the government's racial equality minister in 2006, Philip Woolas, had called for her dismissal, accusing her of "denying the right of children to a full education" because her stand meant she could not 'do her job' and insisted that barring men from working with her would amount to 'sexual discrimination'.[74]

Azmi contested her dismissal at the Employment Appeals Tribunal in London, although she was publicly advised by Labour MP Shahid Malik to drop the case. Her legal battle coincided with the uproar and debate triggered by Jack Straw's comments in which he revealed that he asked Muslim women visiting his constituency surgeries to consider uncovering their faces to allow better communication. Pictures of Azmi in full *niqab* could be found on the front pages of all major newspapers.

Her claim of religious discrimination was brought as a test case under the new religious discrimination regulations, The Employment Equality (religion or belief) Regulations 2004. There appeared to be religio-political forces influencing her legal battle. Some news reports claimed that she acted on the advice of a *fatwa* from mufti Yusuf Sacha, a Tablighi Jama'at cleric and imam of the Dewsbury mosque which declared that the face-veil is binding on all Muslim women outside the home. The Tablighi Jama'at is a transnational organisation that runs a global Islamic missionary movement. However, it has come under criticism in many Muslim-majority and non-Muslim countries for promoting a hardline, *Deobandi* interpretation of Islam and gender roles. This rumour of links with the Tablighi Jama'at may not be unfounded given that Azmi's father was the headmaster of the Islamic seminary (madrasah) attached to Dewsbury's Markazi mosque. The Markazi mosque is the European Headquarter of the Tablighi Jama'at.[75]

On 30 March 2007, the Employment Appeal Tribunal dismissed Azmi's appeal. It upheld Azmi's right to wear the *niqab* in public places, but maintained that the school had the right to terminate her services as a teacher, in the best interests of the children enrolled in it. As such, the Appeal Tribunal maintained that that she was not directly discriminated against because of her religious beliefs.

The issue of the veil, while most contentious in schools, has also come up on university campuses. In the aftermath of the London 7/7 bombings in July 2005, Imperial College London banned the *niqab* citing security reasons. It clarified that it banned all clothing that covers the face and prevents an individual from being identified. A college spokeswoman said:

> We are absolutely not banning people who wear the *hijab* because the headscarf does not cover the face. We welcome diversity at Imperial College and *hijabs*, *turbans* and other items of clothing that represent this diversity are very welcome.[76]

When these cases were reported in the media, opinion was divided within the Muslim community regarding the place for *niqabs* and *jilbabs* in schools. The Muslim Council of Britain's official policy is that headscarves fulfil the religious requirements of Muslim girls sufficiently. However, there are many members of the community who vocally reject *niqab* as a religious requirement that needs to be accommodated in British educational institutions. The Muslim Educational Centre of Oxford (MECO) terms *niqabs* as 'primitive un-Islamic full face-masks.' In a rare, unprecedented move in February 2007, MECO offered to financially support the defence case of the Buckinghamshire state school against a young Muslim student challenging the school to allow her to wear the *niqab*. MECO is campaigning for the formal banning of the *niqab* from British schools. In a bold press release, the organisation not only sided with the school authorities but also highlighted the larger political forces at play, and the symbolic value assigned to veiling in the Islamist political agenda, stating:

> In connection with recent media reports that the misguided father of a young pupil in Buckinghamshire is seeking a judicial review so that his daughter can wear the face-veil (*niqab*), MECO is on record to robustly resist this non-Islamic imposition upon any British state-funded institution. We are committed to offering the school's principal and staff our full and unequivocal support in banning all face-masks at school. We trust any move to implement this kind of ethnic fringe obsession will be resisted, as it has no foundation within the transcendent sources of Islamic law.
>
> Since the school's dress code already gives Muslim girls the option to wear the headscarf (*hijab*), there is no need for full-face covering. The *niqab*, as all Muslims should know, is a cultural, class-based, pre-Islamic custom and is a un-Qur'anic innovation. Unfortunately, this non-Qur'anic garment is witnessing a contemporary resurgence due to the potency of Saudi petro-dollars, which is influencing fanatical *Wahhabi* theology and its Indo-Pakistani variants here and abroad. However, for Muslims to claim that it is a religious requirement for women (and girls) to conceal their faces while in public is both incorrect and disingenuous, as there is no scriptural authority at all for this chauvinistic perspective....
>
> UK Muslims need to do more to integrate fully into British society, instead of their predilection to divorce themselves from the mainstream by leading segregationist lives.[77]

There are many Muslims and non-Muslims who share MECO's reservations and concerns about the growing power of the *Wahhabi* ideology in Britain. The above survey of the most high-profile legal battles fought over dress codes reveals the nuances of the debate, the (sometimes contradictory) reactions of the state authorities as well as the diversity of opinion among the Muslim community. It is obvious that where these young girls and women have asserted their demand to observe the *niqab* or *jilbab*, there have always been Muslim male backers compelling them to endure complicated legal battles. These men have tended to be from the immediate family, whether fathers or brothers, and appear to be affiliated with transnational Islamist groups. For some secularists and feminists, these connections beg the question of the oft-repeated word 'choice'; to what extent are (veiled) British Muslim women, especially young girls, genuinely exercising choice in following such dress codes?

Others, from within and beyond the community, dismiss these cases, considering them to be the problem of a very tiny minority within the British Muslim community. However, the fact that so much attention is given to it by both sides, is testimony that it is an important issue and needs to be subjected to a more profound analysis.

What is equally clear is that while the language of human rights, and in particular the right to freedom of religious practice, is used by these women, it is noteworthy that their supporters are almost always their fathers or brothers. For an issue that is about women's dress, one would expect to see their mothers or sisters by their sides coming out of courts and tribunals.

Are these women demonstrating agency? Or, are they simply being used by Muslim men seeking the same old patriarchal control over women's bodies?

In the context of the links drawn with transnational movements such as the Hizb ut-Tahrir or the Tablighi Jama'at, have women already been successfully co-opted into spreading fundamentalisms?

6.2 Discrimination in the Labour Market

Muslim women in the UK, like other minorities, face intersecting discrimination on the basis of their minority religious status and as women in their own communities. While strict control of sexuality and physical mobility (including the right to work) by family members (often male) is one reason for the lower participation of Muslim women in the labour force compared to other communities/the national average, dress codes also curtail women's employment opportunities in the UK.

Numerous studies have highlighted evidence of this triple prejudice working against veiled Muslim women in the workforce[78]. Overall, Muslim women have the lowest rates of economic activity in the UK; with more than seven in ten women of working age outside the workforce, their unemployment rate of 18%, is higher than that of any other group[79]. The 2005 Fawcett Society report on BME (a widely used acronym for 'black ethnic minority') women confirmed that women from Pakistani and Bangladeshi communities are the most socially excluded[80]. Women belonging to these ethnic backgrounds find it harder than white British women with the same qualifications to get a job as they are confronted with discrimination on grounds of sex, race and ethnicity and religion[81] with employers assuming that Muslim women will not fit in or will present the wrong image to customers if they wear the *hijab*. Most of these studies, such as the two-year research conducted by the Equal Opportunities Commission (EOC) in September 2006, highlight the wide gap between the aspirations of highly qualified, veiled Muslim women and the career opportunities available to them. According to Jenny Watson, chair of the EOC,

> …Young Pakistani and Bangladeshi girls (are) more ambitious than white girls in the same school. They are more likely to aspire to senior positions and more likely to be graduates. The flipside is that they do experience negative attitudes because of religious dress and are having to take jobs at lower levels than they are qualified for. They are clearly experiencing a mixture of racism and sexism that is difficult to navigate.[82]

Most of the women interviewed in EOC's research complained of a gap between their self perception and the way potential employers saw them. Many cited their preference for adhering to varying religious dress codes (mainly the *hijab*) as a barrier to their acceptance in the workplace on equal terms with other women employees. The EOC reports:

> 1 in 5 Pakistani and Bangladeshi women had *often/sometimes* experienced negative attitudes at work for wearing religious dress. Given that over 90% of Pakistani and Bangladeshi women are Muslim, and some wear the *hijab*, we can infer that some negative attitudes apply to this form of religious dress. This is an extra layer of difficulty faced by some Pakistani and Bangladeshi women on the basis of their faith. (Botcherby: 2006, p.14)

Such findings are also corroborated by newspaper articles as well as personal interviews conducted for this research. Most of the women interviewed informed the author that they were often faced with questions from their peers and superiors about their headscarf in the workplace. Not all questions were out of genuine curiosity, however. Many questions and remarks tended to be hostile. The *hijab* is experienced as a barrier not only when competing for a job placement but also for later upward mobility in organisations. The glass ceiling for them can be lower than for non-Muslim, non-veiled women.

For example, twenty-nine year old Saeeda Ahmed describes how her interviewer viewed her *hijab* during a job interview at an investment bank in Bradford:

> He just looked at me. He almost didn't want to talk to me. On paper I came across as ambitious, motivated and experienced, but when he saw the way I looked he just thought, 'No, she doesn't fit in with this organisation.[83]

Another twenty-nine year old British Muslim woman of Bangladeshi background, Mandy, narrated her experience of wearing *shalwar kameez* in an arts organisation as follows:

> In the first week, I was wearing my *shalwar kameez* with a shawl. The manager said, 'You look like a Taliban terrorist.' I asked him why he said that and he told me we Muslims were too sensitive and needed to lighten up. I was the only Muslim woman. There was a culture of ignoring it so everyone became complicit in the treatment.[84]

Dr. David Tyrer and Fauzia Ahmed's summary report on 'Muslim Women and Higher Education: Identities, Experiences and Prospects', launched in 2006 at the Institute of Education, highlights the extent to which these 'visibly Muslim women' experience discrimination in the labour market despite the huge investments they make in education.[85] It highlighted their aspirations, the attitudes of some employers towards women from Muslim backgrounds and the reality that reaching the 'top' (management positions) was still incredibly difficult for women from ethnic minority backgrounds. "The EOC research came up with a contradictory finding that whereas *hijab*-wearing Muslim women see their *hijab* as a factor contributing to discrimination against them in employment, employers said that they did not view *hijab* as being problematic."[86]

This issue was significant enough to be raised in a Muslim women's special meeting with the Prime Minister in May 2006, where one participant said:

> Wearing *hijab* can be a barrier to Muslim women gaining employment as employers see the *hijab*, not the person. You have to prove you are better than others when you wear *hijab*. Although there are plenty of anti-discrimination

and equal opportunities policies, they are not practised. If more women are seen in the public-eye wearing *hijab*, it would encourage other Muslim women to put themselves forward.[87]

While the limited number of interviews conducted for this paper comprised women who chose to wear the *hijab* of their own free will, often after the age of 19 and without having similar precedents in their immediate families, not all British Muslim women can be assumed to exercise free choice in the matter of dress. From the author's discussions with the Muslim community, it seems it is highly probable that Muslim women in the Midlands (Bradford, Birmingham, Leicester) and even certain parts of London (Southall, East London) have to challenge their families to be able to exercise their right to work and realise their ambitions. They often negotiate these choices by using their own knowledge of Islam to challenge gender stereotypes and roles imposed on them by their families and wider community. Religious adherence (and indeed associated dress codes) is then experienced as a liberating force against community pressures, allowing them to enjoy the benefits of individual freedoms offered as a consequence of living in a western society, while retaining the coveted respect of their community.

Having secured community support for participating in the workforce, on terms that are unfamiliar/traditionally unacceptable to their community, such women are then faced with reluctant employers who are unwilling to accept their *hijab*.

This has become a source of concern for the women who find themselves caught between their career aspirations and giving up their religious practices and with it the legitimating acceptance of the community. Many seek the advice of local imams such as Sheikh Ibrahim Mogra on how they should respond when faced with a prospective employer's explicit request that they remove the *hijab* as a pre-condition for employment. According to Mogra, this dilemma is not restricted to any single profession, but is experienced by veiled Muslim women applying for positions in small retail businesses to large financial corporations. Mogra explained that he advises women to retain the *hijab* and offers to negotiate with the company on her behalf (either individually or under the leadership of the MCB). This is a traditional approach where a male 'guardian' represents the interest of and speaks on behalf of women, within the public sphere.

He cited his consultation with Boots Pharmaceutical company, Next and IKEA as successful examples of negotiation where the companies incorporated the headscarf as a uniform option for Muslim women employers and designed them on MCB's recommendations. These organisations included their logos on the headscarf so that it fitted in with their uniform and corporate image. He cited other such examples set by the Metropolitan Police (of London), the Army and the Ministry of Defence who have incorporated the *hijab* as an approved uniform option for women employees and a trimmed beard for Muslim men.

Nevertheless, Mogra expressed his disappointment with companies who didn't show such flexibility in accommodating these dress code preferences:

> On the one hand, the 'west' is very critical of Muslim women staying at home but then at the same time they are unwilling to accommodate Muslim women who want to work while retaining their *hijab*… this is a very dangerous trend because it has a chain dynamic, pushing Muslim communities further into economic disadvantage and deprivation… [with the result that] the British workforce would then *not* reflect the true diversity of this nation by keeping Muslim women out of the labour market, simply because of the way they dress. (I. Mogra, personal communication, 17 August 2006)

Mogra emphasised that in all negotiations with companies and the government, Muslim organisations should not be seen as rigid and irrational. They should instead be "flexible but without compromising on principle". He explained that with the enforcement of the Employment Equality (Religion or Belief) Regulations since 2 December 2003, British Muslims could now legally contest such cases of discrimination. This law provides direct protection from religious discrimination in employment and vocational training from which Muslims can also benefit. This protection was previously lacking, especially for Muslims who were not able to seek judicial redress to religion-based discrimination under the Race Relations Act of 1976.

The 2003 Regulations ban 'direct' and 'indirect' forms of discrimination on the grounds of an individual's religion, in employment and vocational training. The law provides protection during the process of recruitment and interviews and in relation to pay, terms and conditions of employment, training, promotion and dismissal and the provision of references. The Regulations' second provision of 'Indirect Discrimination' pertains directly to issues of dress codes. If an employer has a rule or policy which applies to everyone, but which in practice, disadvantages members of a particular religion, this amounts to indirect discrimination. In its public advocacy guide on the subject, the MCB states:

A classic example is where an employer has a uniform policy that women must wear knee length skirts. The only defence available to an employer is to show that the rule is in place to meet a legitimate aim and that no other less damaging alternative would meet that aim.

So legally, such dress policies, which effectively exclude Muslim women who do not wish to conform to them on the basis of their faith or politics, can only be justified if it is absolutely essential to the nature of the business involved, or on health and safety grounds. As a general principle, employers are now expected to accommodate 'Muslim' dress codes.

In the public sector, the main example of a best practice that meets MCB's gender ideology in this respect is the Metropolitan Police of London. In a move to meet recruitment targets under the 'Protect and Respect' diversity strategy adopted to help the force reflect the ethnic composition of the city it serves[88], the Metropolitan Police introduced a headscarf and an ankle length gown as an alternative uniform option for women officers in 2001 (the decision was announced on 25 April 2001). The London Metropolitan Police commissioned four designs and decided upon a distinctive Metropolitan Police black and white cheque pattern. This step was taken in response to a long-standing demand from several Muslim officers, as well a proposal submitted to the then Metropolitan Police Commissioner, Sir John Stevens, in February 2001[89].

Many Muslim police officers welcomed this measure, hoping that it would encourage more Muslim women into the police force who had been deterred by the prospect of not being allowed to wear headscarves with their uniform. It is noteworthy to mention here that Britain's Sikh community had already won the right to wear their traditional *turban* on police duty before 2001.

In the private sector, one of the companies which took special steps to incorporate Muslim veiling practices is the international, Swedish household goods retailer IKEA. In 2005, IKEA's Edmonton branch (in London) commissioned TheHijabShop.com to design and produce a *hijab* that would match their uniform. British Airways is another major company which allows for religious apparel to be worn in the workplace including Sikh *turbans* and Muslim headscarves.

Recently, demands for the accommodation of a so-called Muslim dress code were heard in the medical profession as well. In June 2006, a medical student of the University of St. Andrews, Sabrina Talukdar, raised the issue at the British Medical

Association's conference in Manchester, calling for hospitals to allow Muslim women to wear a 'theatre *hijab*' in operation theatres. Talukdar complained that presently, there was no standard practice in the UK on this issue. She said that while some hospitals insisted staff take *hijab* off during surgery, others allowed them to cover it with surgical headgear. (Outside the theatre, NHS[90] staff are free to wear religious dress according to their preferences.) However, according to Talukdar, failure to respect cultural values in the operating theatre was discouraging women from entering the medical profession.

Ms. Talukdar suggested that to ensure an infection-free environment for the patients, the *hijab* could be made from sterile material. In addition to dress codes, she also suggested putting up screens to shield Muslim women from male colleagues when washing or cleansing before an operation.

This demand seems to be an isolated case. It was based on an assumption that such gender segregation is a Muslim or Islamic requirement and she was able to make this case successfully under the banner of multiculturalism. However, it must be noted that Muslim women doctors in many Muslim-majority countries do not veil and have not demanded separate hand-washing facilities before surgery. Therefore, the claim that this is an Islamic requirement is itself, contentious.

Participants at the conference, however, responded favourably to this concern raised by the Muslim student and passed a motion that NHS and medical schools should accommodate religious practices of staff and students as long as patient care was not compromised[91]. The outcome of this motion and its applicability to NHS facilities is yet to be seen.

Those who are in favour of women's veiling no doubt celebrate these victories as the success of multiculturalism, minority rights and women's right to choose. However, when does this choice – which for now enhances women's access to the labour force – become a compulsion? When will colleagues start pressurising other women who choose not to veil?

Many a lesson should be learnt from other contexts where fundamentalist ideologies and movements easily – and often discreetly – transform themselves from a mere presence in society (which starts by increasing options for religious observance or affiliation) into a source of compulsion, and ultimately, a violation of rights. At a micro level, the peer pressure and explicit instruction from teachers to veil has already been witnessed in several Islamic preaching organisations such as Al-Huda and even in the more informal *tafseer* and *dars* lessons.

6.3 Competing for Sports Facilities

In 2001, Britain became the first non-Muslim country to attend the (fourth) Women's Islamic Games in Tehran, Iran. The British team participated for the second time in 'futsal' (five-a-side football) at the September 2005 event under the sponsorship of the *Muslim News*[92] which set up the Muslim Women's Sport Foundation (MWSF) in London.

The MWSF is a response to the extremely low level of Muslim women's participation in a variety of sports in the UK. Some 39% of women in Britain take part in sports as opposed to only 19% of British women of Indian, Pakistani and Bangladeshi origin. On the one hand, the MWSF provides an acceptable and conducive space to those young girls who may not be able to realise their sporting ambitions in conventional settings, due to parental opposition. On the other hand, it provides an alternative route for ambitious sportswomen/athletes who reject or are rejected by the mainstream women's national teams on account of their dress code preference. For instance, one member of the British Muslim Women's squad joined the team after being rejected by her university's football team which had asked her to remove her headscarf when playing for the team. According to Elham Buaras of the *Muslim News*:

> A girl should not have to decide whether to follow her religion or the sport she loves. If a Muslim girl wants to wear a *hijab*, because she believes it is a religious prescription, she should be free to do so.[93]

The MWSF was established in 2001 by Ahmed Versi (editor of the *Muslim News*) to encourage Muslim women's participation in sports without compromising their religious beliefs. Versi recounted his motivation for setting up the Foundation as follows:

> I once went to Iran when Faiza Hashmi had just won the elections and so I interviewed 3 women in that trip: one was the Advisor on women's issues, another was Shela from Zanan Magazine and the third was of course Faiza Hashmi herself.

Faiza Hashmi was involved in women in sports at the time - they had Muslim women from Muslim countries playing. So I asked her: what about Muslim women from non-Muslim countries? So in their Annual General Meeting in 2001 in London, they changed their constitution to allow Muslim women from non-Muslim countries to participate as well.

So we advertised heavily in the papers, through our own paper (the *Muslim News*), that here are the International Women's Islamic Games now open to British Muslim women – it's all female, everything takes place in all-women environment. (A. Versi, personal communication, 23 July 2008)

Versi received an overwhelming response from the Muslim community to the advertisements which suggested to him that (veiled) British Muslim women did indeed want to participate in competitive sports.

Versi continued:

We only had 2 to 3 months to prepare teams for the International [Islamic Women's] Games so we didn't obviously have much time. We took the futsal and badminton [team]. We didn't have good enough players for other games.

You must keep in mind that the International Games at that time were very political as well – 9/11 had just happened, there was talk of bombing Afghanistan…. We went against the advice of the Foreign Office. Of course we lost badly, but that was expected. I mean the oldest person in our badminton team was 50 years and the youngest in the futsal team was 15. So you can imagine the age difference and the team. (A. Versi, personal communication, 23 July 2008)

Although both teams secured only a fair play award, the British players thoroughly enjoyed their experience. Versi proudly exclaimed: "It was such an honour you know because when we entered the stadium, three countries got a standing applause: Iran (the host), Afghanistan and the UK. Can you imagine the British flag getting such a response in Iran?"

Rimla Akhtar, Chairperson of the Foundation led the futsal team at the Games and fondly remembers the 'friendly atmosphere' which gave Muslim women from all over the world the chance to get to know each other.

After returning from the International Games, Versi decided to set up the Muslim Women's Sports Foundation as a non-profit organisation with the aim of encouraging British Muslim women to participate in sports. Eight years on, the Foundation continues to be run by volunteers, all of whom have a passion for sports but are also pursuing other careers. The Foundation acts as the official representative of the International Women's Islamic Games for Britain. Versi is now an Advisor to the Foundation and is encouraging the girls to take the lead in looking after its day-to-day management. He was nominated to be a member of the Games' Executive Committee representing the only non-Muslim country vote.

Versi said that he is very keen to promote Muslim women's participation in sports in other non-Muslim countries. But he complained that none of his letters to any Muslim organisation across Europe got any response.

Explaining the need for the Foundation in Britain, Versi said:

> In this country, because there's a problem with the *hijab* and all the referees are male, Muslim girls don't want to play sports. I will tell you one example: there was a girl – a very bright student – who played football wearing *hijab* and tracks. The referee asked her to leave the ground because she was wearing (the) *hijab*. We did a campaign then that universities should let any women with [religious] dress codes play. (A. Versi, personal communication, 23 July 2008)

Versi said that as most coaches tend to be male, it is very difficult to build the calibre of the Muslim women's teams to compete at the national level, as they often do not want to be trained by men. In response, the Foundation is undertaking to train some Muslim women to be coaches.

The MWSF now has regular weekly training sessions for basketball and futsal in London and Birmingham. Members (players) pay a token fee of £6 per month which helps to cover the cost of the coaches. The London training sessions are held in the indoor sports hall of the Harrow High School – the Foundation successfully negotiated with the Harrow Council to allow them to use the facilities free of cost. This location, as opposed to the previous one – a hall in Watford High School (further towards North West London) – has important advantages for the membership, explained Ayesha Abdeen, the Vice Chairman of the Foundation responsible for Sports Development and Regional Promotions. Abdeen explained that their strategy to attract new players from the community was to facilitate the removal of barriers preventing veiled British Muslim women from participating in sports and to meet them on their terms. She cited mobility restrictions as a major barrier for Muslim women as their families "are not comfortable with them travelling long distances alone, or going to areas they are not familiar with, even if it's just half an hour away." The other main barriers she cited are: dress including *hijab* and full length tracks, women-only facilities and female coaches.

While not veiled herself, Abdeen was very sensitive to other women's desire to retain their headscarf or wear tracksuits when playing and asserted that this requirement should not pose a barrier for them. Born to Sri Lankan parents, Abdeen is a trained physiotherapist and runs a small family business. She played for a sports academy in the Richmond area of South West London for several years before deciding to give it up. Explaining her motivation to leave the academy despite being such a successful player, she said:

> To be honest with you, I never really fitted in there. Sure, I played well and on the ground I enjoyed the game, but then after every game, I had to go the pub with them. And if you don't drink, you're automatically excluded from the fun. So I thought that this Foundation, here I can be myself. There is no pressure to engage in any activity which I feel is not in line with my religion and I think many of the girls who come here, feel the same thing. Their parents and families are also comfortable with the idea because they know they are hanging out with Muslims as opposed to being in a pub. (A. Abdeen, personal communication, 3 August 2008)

Rimla Akhtar, the Chairperson, is a qualified Chartered Accountant and holds a full-time job as an Associate at Price Waterhouse Coopers. Akhtar highlighted the great lengths which they have to go to in order to accommodate the needs of their fellow players. A particular area of difficulty was finding appropriate venues for practice. Apparently, most Muslim girls and women only want to play sports in indoor halls without any windows to ensure that no men can see them. Akhtar said that in order to appease worried parents, they welcome them to visit the venue themselves. She believes in working closely with the community – not just the women, but also their mothers and fathers – to bring about a change in their perspective. She said that while she and many members of the MWSF Executive Committee may not have faced such barriers themselves, if they were to be successful in encouraging Muslim girls to dream of pursuing sports, they needed to keep advocating for provision of appropriate facilities for women.

While the goals of the Foundation are ambitious in that they are a pioneering organisation calling for women to participate in competitive sports, they face severe funding challenges. Akhtar remains hopeful,

> Going forward, I think if we have survived the first eight years which were the most difficult, we will be able to make it... it is difficult, but we are that crazy about sports! (R. Akhtar, personal communication, 2 August 2008)

Akhtar and Abdeen highlighted their plans of promoting sports for Muslim women by touring across the country and holding Fun Days. They were sensitive to the challenges they faced from within the community which strictly de-prioritises women's sports:

> Our mothers' generation only had the option of staying at home and raising a family. Our generation has more options but although we can have a career now, we are still not doing any sports. Hopefully the next generation will be able to have both. That is what we are trying to do – to sort of lay the foundation for them. (A. Abdeen, personal communication, 2 August 2008)

The Foundation plans to launch a health education project targeting Muslim students in schools to sensitise them about the need for exercise and a healthy lifestyle. Akhtar said that the Foundation recognised that for Muslim girls to believe that sports were something they could do, they had to be socialised from early childhood. Recalling her own experience, she said, "I was doing sports the minute I started walking. My mother really encouraged me to play sports from the beginning because she too, was very sporty as a girl. In fact, she is the one who pushed me to try out for the International Women's Islamic Games trials in 2001! But if you look around, the vast majority of Muslim girls are not taught to catch the ball as a toddler...with the result that when they come to us, we have to start coaching them from a very basic level."

These two Executive Committee members were highly enthusiastic and ambitious about their plans for the Foundation and for British Muslim women. They aimed to bring Muslim women into mainstream sports, to be able to compete at the national level and one day play in the Olympic Games. They saw themselves as role models for the next generation.

The MWSF has taken the lead in advocating for changes in the Football Association's (FA) prescribed rules for uniform. At present, the official FA uniform kit guidelines do not allow for any headscarf or long tracks (to cover the legs) to be worn by the players. Citing health and safety reasons, it bans any headgear and, as such neither the headscarf nor the turban can be allowed on the field. The Foundation protests against this guideline, emphasising that such prescriptions prevent Muslim women (who cover themselves) from participating in sports.

The Foundation is actively trying to link up with several other local level Muslim women's sports groups and aims to facilitate their players' sports development. Towards this end, it routinely holds joint practice sessions with the 'Elite Youth', in the Tower Hamlets of East London.

Initiatives like the MWSF are important in enabling British Muslim women to take up sports as a professional career or even to publicly advocate in the community in favour of Muslim girls' participation in sports. At present, they face a tremendous number of barriers from their families and community. Most parents and male family members discourage girls' enthusiasm for sports. Most girls are only able to actively do sports while at school when it is compulsory. These concerns are closely linked to notions of (modesty and) appropriate dress codes. As Shahed Saleh, a young British Muslim with five sisters explains:

> I wouldn't want them (my sisters) to play sports. You're not allowed to uncover yourself like wearing tracksuit bottoms and all that, and play football or badminton, you have to cover yourself. [94]

These attitudes – along with their religious justifications – prevent girls from taking part in sports beyond puberty or late teens. In the same news item which reported Shahid Saleh's views quoted above, an eighteen year old girl, Raheema from Tower Hamlets (east London), which has a large Muslim majority, said that she only played badminton in her backyard. She was not encouraged to do any sport by her family who would much rather see her doing household chores. She had not been allowed to go swimming after the age of twelve because "no Muslim girl can wear a revealing swimming costume."

Such obstacles are overcome by forums such as MWSF where Muslim girls can express their sports ambitions without violating their (or their families') religious beliefs about gender roles. At the competitions that they compete in and the places where they practice and train for such events, they observe 'modest' religious dress codes (often a *hijab* and loose t-shirt and tracks not revealing anything except the face and the hands) and do not play in front of men. For girls like Faiza Akmal, being part of the British Muslim Women's futsal squad had enabled her to play sport in an environment that did not contradict her religion: "I am able to show the general British public that Muslim women are empowered."

As Samana Fazel, another member of team very aptly expressed:

> These Games have given me the opportunity to represent who I am – a British Muslim – while playing a sport that I love. We all [the Squad] understand the importance of our roles and the way in which we can shape the future of sport in the lives of Muslim women all around the country. It's a great honour and a great responsibility. [95]

In many ways, the creation of the Muslim Women's Sports Foundation was a major breakthrough for challenging but also overcoming the multiple barriers faced by British Muslim women seeking to participate in sports. Since 2001, several government and sports governing bodies have recognised the issue in their reports, some of which call for a greater sensitivity to so-called Muslim dress codes. Rimla Akhtar and Ayesha Abdeen's efforts were paramount in generating this understanding for they have proactively networked with all major sport governing bodies in the UK and routinely make presentations to them about the needs of British Muslim women.

Since then, and perhaps inspired by the MWSF, a number of smaller local level initiatives have been made by Muslim women to set up alternative facilities for themselves. One such initiative is the Sisters Games, located in Birmingham. While this group has been showcased in a report by the Women's Sports Foundation, its aims are not as ambitious as those of the MWSF. The Sisters Games was set up by Shalina and her husband, Amin, to advertise and facilitate sports events for Muslim women in the Birmingham area. In an interview with the author, she said that the inspiration to set it up was spontaneous as she, a twenty-five year-old mother of two, discovered one day that she had nowhere suitable to exercise in her local area: "There was no gym where there's no camera or window and where I could take my *hijab* off. There isn't really much out there for Muslim women."

So her husband supported her decision to distribute leaflets (in bookstores and door-to-door) and to set up a website to advertise their initiative. Shalina said that it is still very informal. They essentially rent a hall where women can play indoor badminton and football and also exercise. The age group of the regular members ranges from 22 to 30 years, comprising mothers, housewives, students and professionals of mainly

Bangladeshi and Pakistani origin. Explaining the motivation of her members to use her facilities, Shalina said:

> We provide a secure environment. Everyone who comes to my place wears a *hijab* or *niqab* – some even wear a *burqa* – they ask me ten times: is the door locked? People have a right to be strict, to follow their religion. (Shalina, personal communication, 23 July 2008)

This comment denotes a certain level of anxiety on the part of the users of the exercise facilities about not wanting to be seen without a veil by non-*mahram* men who may accidently open the door.

Shalina is of Bangladeshi origin and was brought up in Bangladesh and completed her GCSE from there before coming to the UK. She is educated up to A' Level.

The latest Muslim sports initiative to capture media attention was the 2007 launch of 'The Ninjabis'. Organised by the Islamic Circles, 'The Ninjabi' project cleverly turns the stereotype of the submissive and timid Muslim women on its head by creating a hybrid of the word ninja and *hijabi*. The classes are taken by a female instructor, Dee Terret, who while not a Muslim herself, supports the vision of the project.

The classes are offered in the heart of a large East London Muslim community in Manor Park. The project has four levels, the titles of which aptly reflect the influence of Hollywood Bruce Lee films on the present generation of British Muslims:

1. Enter the Ninjabi;
2. Return of the Ninjabi;
3. Way of the Ninjabi;
4. Fist of the Ninjabi.

The emergence of such women-only sports groups providing facilities sensitive to some British Muslim women's dress codes and other needs indicates a cultural shift. The £160 billion-a-year global sportswear industry has begun to take notice of the consumer power of the 650 million Muslim women in the world. In 2006, Nike partnered with the United Nations to design a new product: a volleyball uniform for veiled Somalian women which allowed them to play with their heads and bodies covered. An Australian designer, Abeda Zanetti, has designed the popular 'hijood'

– a *hijab* shaped like a hood, which is simple to wear and affords easier mobility to Muslim sportswomen[96].

In the city of London alone, there are 296,606 Muslim women.[97] The economic clout of the present generation of British Muslim women has created the demand for more sports and exercise facilities for women who cover, and their social capital has ensured that the need is being met.

This chapter has canvassed some of the key arenas where British Muslim women are using the veil and religion to carve out a space for themselves outside the home. While they have secured some vital gains in these efforts, to what extent is this a successful strategy for the long-term and what consequences will it have for women's options in the future?

Will the visible increase in veils in private offices, public sector institutions and schools compromise the principles of secularism upheld in Britain? Will the 'freedom to veil' eventually transform into peer pressure on unveiled British Muslim women to cover up? These fears are not unique to the British case, but are also raised in the debate on religious dress codes in Turkey by many secular feminists. These debates are covered in the following chapter, 'The View from Europe.'

Chapter 7: The View from Europe

Muslim women's dress codes are a source of concern beyond the United Kingdom, in Ireland and continental Europe as well. The British Muslim community has closely followed the debates vis à vis the *hijab* and *niqab* in Europe, particularly those surrounding the 2004 French ban on religious symbols in French state schools. Indeed, that year, the London-based Islamic Human Rights Commission (IHRC)[98], documenting attempts to pass legislation barring the headscarf in several European countries, stated that, "Muslim women in Europe have become the latest targets of resurgent prejudice that combines misogynistic precepts with racist and Islamophobic rhetoric" (Ansari & Karim: 2004, p.3)[99]. The IHRC used references to national legislation in specific European countries as well as regional legislation under the European Convention on Human Rights (ECHR) and international treaties like the Universal Declaration of Human Rights 1948 (UDHR) and the UN Declaration on the Elimination of All Forms of Intolerance and of Discrimination Based on Religious Belief (1981 Declaration) to challenge attempts at banning the headscarf from public institutions by various European governments. This is evidence of the increasing cooptation of human rights discourse and language by forces ideologically opposed to gender equality and also fundamentalist groups. The IHRC is a faith-based group whose annual report (2008) explicitly states that it derives inspiration from 'Qur'anic injunctions'[100].

These events in Europe have been significant enough to prompt a response from the British Muslim population and also fuelled a debate on the Muslim women's dress codes in Britain. While the scope of this research does not extend to providing a thorough comparative analysis of all European countries, this chapter canvasses the key elements of the discourses heard in Ireland, France, Germany, Sweden and Turkey and the lessons that can be drawn from these varying contexts.

7.1 Republic of Ireland
There are approximately 32,539 Muslims in the Republic of Ireland out of the country's total population of 4,156,119 people (2006 census). The Muslim population grew rapidly between 1991 and 2002 recording a quadruple rise from 3,873 to 19,147. Unlike the UK, the curious point to note about the ethnic composition of the Muslim population in Ireland, is that nearly a third of this minority is white Irish (i.e. converts to Islam). The rest of the community comprises of diverse ethnicities. The dominant sect is Sunni.

Ireland's first significant wave of migration of Muslims dates back to the 1950s, when many people from the Arab states come to the country as students or businessmen. Unlike the UK, the Republic of Ireland did not have any labour treaties with the former British colonies. Like the UK, uniform policies are not formed by the Department of Education and come under the jurisdiction of individual schools' governing authorities. However, it differs from the UK as both its Constitution and its Equal Status Act 2000 prohibit discrimination on the basis of religious belief in the provision of goods, services and facilities. Its Employment Equality Act similarly outlaws discrimination in employment on grounds of religious belief.

The implementation of this legislation has been supported by the establishment of the Equality Authority which works to promote equality of opportunity guaranteed under these laws and to raise public awareness of the protection offered by them. The Authority has successfully resolved several incidents where Muslim schoolgirls have been denied access to education because of their wearing of the headscarf. In such cases, the Authority intervened to uphold these schoolgirls' right to wear the headscarf and advised the schools of the illegality of their practice under the law.

However, the lack of official guidance on uniform rules from the Department of Education created much confusion for individual school administrations in deciding whether headscarves could be permitted in the classroom. The Department of Education maintains that it provided its policy on students' Muslim dress codes in a letter to a Dublin school in 2005 where it advised the teacher to allow a student to wear the *hijab* during PE. This contrasted with the same Department's advice to Goery Community School in 2007 where the latter was told that it was up to the school's board of management to decide whether students could wear the *hijab*. The present Education Minister has requested Conor Lenihan, who was appointed Minister of State with special responsibility for Integration Policy in June 2007, to address this issue of dress codes in a new policy document, the Intercultural Education Strategy.

In contrast with the steps taken by school administrations in England, the two examples from the Republic of Ireland show schools' principles proactively seeking advice from the Department of Education in matters of students' dress codes in the absence of any coherent uniform guidelines. However, the apparent u-turn in the Department's advice to schools may be due to the politicisation of the issue in recent years. Liam Egan, the father of the girl from Gorey Community School whose wearing of the *hijab* prompted her principle to solicit the advice of the Department, is suspicious:

The law has not changed, so why has the department changed its position? Since 7/7 this has become more of a political issue. My daughter wore the *hijab* all through her first year in school and it was not contentious. Then, at the end of the year, it suddenly became an issue.

In protest, Egan decided to help in establishing the Irish Hijab Campaign to lobby for the rights of female Muslim students to wear the *hijab*. The Campaign dismisses as baseless the common fears or argument against the *hijab* that the next step is the *niqab* or *burqa*.

An interesting dimension to the politics of the veil in Ireland is the fact that more than one-third of all its Muslim population is native Irish. As such, Egan asserts that "this is not an immigrant issue. It's about freedom to practice religious beliefs. People say we should assimilate, but I was born in Wexford – I am Irish and Muslim."

While Egan made the above comments to a reporter of The Times, statements of the Irish Hijab Campaign contradict his claim that he is not concerned with the *niqab*. In fact, the minutes of the campaign meeting (held on 12 July 2008) indicate that the group is carefully planning its advocacy strategy to lobby relevant Government ministries to allow *hijabs* in educational institutions without jeopardising any future demand for a similar accommodation of the *niqab*[101].

At present, the Irish Hijab Campaign has 17 men and 7 women members. The members are conscious of the need to recruit more women in order for the Campaign to appear to legitimately represent Muslim women. However, this gender imbalance in a campaign which is about an item of women's clothing, reflects once again, the loud voices of Muslim men claiming to speak on behalf of women. This is not very different from the disproportionate number of male advocates of female Muslim students' right to wear the *niqab* or *jilbab* in English schools.

Ireland was hailed as an example of good practice by the IHRC for its creation of the Racial and Intercultural Office within the Garda Police force, which took the initiative of incorporating the headscarf as a uniform option to encourage Muslim women to join the force. Far from being a response to any demand or pressure from Muslim community representatives, this move was the Garda Office's own initiative.

The Office also supported two Irish Muslim women who were refused passports because they wore the niqab. It managed to resolve the issue in favour of the women after contacting the Department of Justice.

7.2 France

Of metropolitan France's[102] total population of 62,150,775 people, Muslims are estimated to be 3%[103]. With 5 million followers, Islam is the second largest religion in France, after Catholicism. This is a widely cited estimate and should only be used as an indicative figure as France does not collect data about its citizens' religious affiliation in the national census (due to the strong principle of *laïcité* explored below). The North-African (Maghrebian) population is the dominant ethnic group within the French Muslim minority as the table below shows:

Region of Origin	Percentage of Muslim Population
Algeria	37.30%
Morocco	24.07%
Tunisia	8.42%
Turkey	7.58%
Sub-Saharan Africa	6.02%
Middle East	2.41%
Asians (mostly from Pakistan and Bangladesh)	2.41%
Converts	0.96%
Awaiting registration	8.42%
Other	2.41%
Total	**100%**

France has in common with the UK the fact that large numbers of its Muslim immigrants came from its former colonies. However, unlike the integration policy of Britain which promotes multiculturalism, the French system is based on the principles of assimilation complemented by secularism as being crucial to the social harmony and national cohesion of France and her citizens. This strong emphasis on secularism dates back to a 1905 law separating the Church and the State, as well as a series of laws dating back to the early 1880s, which insisted on free, compulsory and secular education.

In September 2004, the French Government under former President Jacques Chirac banned all 'conspicuous' religious symbols from state schools. This was the most significant measure in *l'affaire du voile* (the veil affair)[104] which sparked massive street protests in France and internationally between December 2003 and September

2004. It led to the formation of the Europe-wide campaign, The Assembly for the Protection of Hijab, on 14 June 2004 at the House of Commons in London, at a gathering of prominent MPs, MEPs, human rights organisations and other supporters as mentioned above in the introduction to this chapter.

In France, the controversy over the veil dates back to October 1989, when three female students were suspended for refusing to remove their veils in class at Gabriel Havez Middle School in Creil, France. In November 1989, the Conseil d'Etat supported the students' right to wear the veil on the basis that it did not contradict the secularity of public schools. The following month witnessed a statement by the then Prime Minister Lionel Jospin declaring that educators had the prerogative to permit or refuse headscarves in the classroom on a case-by-case basis[105].

The year 1990 saw similar suspensions of Muslim girls from Pasteur Middle School in Noyon, while the parents of the one of the girls suspended the previous year from Gabriel Havez School filed a defamation lawsuit against its Principal. These events saw the issuance of a second government statement reiterating its position which emphasised respecting the principle of secularity in public schools.

This was followed by a memorandum from the Education Minister in September 1994 called the 'Francois Bayrou memo' which sought to distinguish between 'discreet' religious symbols which could be brought into the classroom and 'ostentatious' religious symbols (including the headscarf) which were to be forbidden in state schools and for all state employees. It discouraged 'ostentatious display of religious allegiance' in state educational facilities. This led to a wide range of reactions, including a broad mobilisation of advocates of the French version of secularism as well as a protest demonstration by students of St. Exupery High School in Mantes-la-Jolie the following month, who supported the right/freedom to wear a veil in classrooms. Nevertheless, twenty-four students (wearing headscarves) were suspended from that school and from Faideherbe High in Lille.

Prior to the 1994 regulation, the State Constitutional Council had ruled that Muslim girl pupils were free to wear headscarves, as long as they continued to respect the rule that no proselytism was allowed on state school premises.

In 1999, teachers and staff of a junior high school in the small town of Flers went on strike when a twelve year old girl of Turkish origin refused to take off her headscarf in the school. The staff, numbering some seventy people, protested that the pupil breached the 1994 regulation. Teachers in another school (in Lyon) were also reported to have staged similar protests when faced with Muslim girls asserting their will to observe the veil in the classroom.

It is estimated that one hundred female students were suspended or expelled from middle and high schools for wearing the veil in the classroom between 1994 and 2003.

In December 2003, President Chirac pursued the recommendation of a commission led by Bernard Stasi to look into the issue and supported a new law to ban 'conspicuous' religious signs from state schools. On 10 February 2004, a bill containing proposals for legislation to this effect was passed in Parliament with 494 votes in its favour, with only 36 against. The bill was also supported by the opposition Socialists at the time. The bill prohibits the wearing of the Muslim headscarf, Jewish *kippa*, Sikh turban and large crucifix in state schools. So far, the ban is limited to state schools only, while headscarves can be worn in Muslim (faith) schools and in universities. The Parliamentary Speaker, Jean-Louis Debre, a member of the then ruling UMP party, declared his support for the bill saying, "What is at issue here is the clear affirmation that public school is a place for learning and not for militant activity or proselytism". The measure received overwhelming political and public support up to 70% according to public opinion polls[106].

Supporters of this ban base their arguments on secularism and feminism. The dominant debate on this issue focuses on the essential secular nature of the French state and institutions. Proponents from the general public as well as government officials have insisted that France's principles of secularism are threatened by what they perceive as assertions of religious identity as exemplified by Muslim women's headscarves in state institutions which are expected to maintain a strict degree of secularism. From the point of view of the French government, adoption/practice of such dress codes is incompatible with the *laïcité* (secularism) which public places are required to uphold. An MP from President Chirac's party, Jacques Myard stated that:

> … [there is a] big difference between discreetly wearing a cross, a hand of Fatima or Star of David round your neck…[and a headscarf which is]… incompatible with the neutrality of the school and the French Republic.[107]

It should be noted here that state schools in France do not offer any religious education and in fact, the teaching of any religion in these schools is prohibited.

The second argument put forth in favour of the ban is based on an understanding of feminism that defines the *hijab* as a symbol of women's oppression and subservience to men. Those subscribing to this view questioned the element of 'free choice' in Muslim girls' decision to observe such dress codes and said that it was usually a result of social pressure. They also raised fears that allowing/accommodating the *hijab* in the classroom could open the door to other practices harmful to women's rights which exist in Muslim-majority societies.

Most girls who fell out of state schools as a result of this law, ended up enrolling in faith schools and distance learning or correspondence courses. IHRC puts this number at 400 (Ansari & Karim: 2004, p.3).

It is a central objective and responsibility of French public schools to train students in Republican values including *laïcité*, and to ensure equal treatment of individual pupils as well as respect for pluralism. As such, local officials have the authority to regulate the public expression of religious affiliation in schools. The conflict over the banning of the *hijab* illustrates the tension between public space and private choices, the difficulties inherent in balancing the requirements of *laïcité* against the needs of veiled Muslim students. In the end, the *hijab* ban can be interpreted as a determined move to maintain a century-long tradition of French secularity over the education system. Unlike Britain, where the debate over the veil is more concerned with full-face veiling (*niqab*) than the *hijab*, France's ban has demonstrated zero tolerance for any headscarf in public schools.

7.3 Germany

Estimated at 3.2 to 3.4 million, Germany has the second largest Muslim population in Western Europe after France; three-quarters are of Turkish origin (approximately 2.5 to 2.6 million) while the rest are immigrants or their descendants from different parts of the world. Those of Turkish origin are not necessarily a homogenous group and are divided along ethnic, class and sectarian lines.

Ideologically, many are influenced by the Kemalist (modernist) tradition where modernist-nationalists interests of the state take precedence over religious affiliation. In this respect and also because they are not former colonial subjects, the history of their migration to Germany is different from that of Muslims who went to France from North Africa or of South Asians who went to Britain. The Turkish community started taking root in Germany through a post-war guest worker programme in 1961. Thousands came to work in low-skilled jobs as seasonal labour in what was then West Germany while East Germany fulfilled its labour requirements by recruiting tens of thousands of workers from Vietnam especially in the 1980s. Due to this historical context of migration, today the Turkish diasporas continue to concentrate in regions of former West Germany.

What further distinguishes the mainly Turkish Muslim community of Germany in their experience as a migrant, minority community from British and French Muslims is their long struggle for citizenship rights. Unlike Britain and France, naturalisation and citizenship were denied to the Turkish migrant workers and their descendants for nearly 40 years. For four decades, permanently resident Turkish citizens were only 'guest workers' or foreigners under German law because Germany never saw itself as a country of immigration. Even second and third generation immigrants (who had been born in the country) were not entitled to German citizenship. Despite denying them citizenship, Germany expected its foreign workers to assimilate into society.

The year 1998 finally saw a dramatic reform of the citizenship law as the Green Coalition was elected to office. The Green Coalition was sympathetic to the demands of the Turkish community and in 1999 a new law was passed which grants citizenship to children born in Germany to non-German parents if at least one parent has been a legal resident for at least five years. Foreigners can now apply for naturalisation after 8 years (for minors) or as long as 15 years (for adults.) The reform, which came into effect in the year 2000, nevertheless fell short of offering citizenship to the millions of foreign residents born before 2000. The law also allowed dual citizenship until the age of 23 years, after which a choice must be made. It should be noted here that the reason why dual citizenship was not offered beyond the age of 23 is that the Government relented to the pressure of a petition campaign in 1999 which collected 5 million signatures to oppose the proposition. This campaign was in fact the largest post-war political mobilisation in Germany.

In 2005, amid much public debate, the southern state of Baden-Württemberg introduced a new two-hour oral exam (dubbed the cultural test) for foreigners wishing to gain German citizenship. Among other questions designed to test loyalty to Germany and suitability to its way of life, the test asks:

> If your adult daughter dressed like a German woman, would you try to prevent her from doing so? [108]

Against this background, it is not surprising that eight out of the 16 states of Germany have banned the headscarf in schools: Baden-Wurttemberg, Bavaria,

Berlin, Bremen, Hesse, Lower Saxony, North Rhine-Westphalia and Saarland. Two of these (namely Hesse and Berlin) have also prohibited civil servants from wearing the headscarf. This has effectively resulted in excluding educated, professional, middle-class German Muslim women from employment opportunities.

In Germany, policies on the use of religious symbols in schools are not regulated by the federal government, but are the jurisdiction of each state. What is interesting about the German case is that the issue of the headscarf arose mainly because of veiled teachers' rather than students.

It is also interesting to note that the laws enacted do not explicitly or exclusively target the headscarf but rather focus on religious symbols. They claim to be concerned about a teacher's external appearance and its impact on the schools strict neutrality. While the states of Bremen and Lower Saxony do not make any exceptions for Christian symbols and Western cultural traditions, the majority of the states (five) with bans do. Human Rights Watch has condemned this and called it "discrimination in the name of equality":

> Those states that ban religious clothing but still allow Christian symbols explicitly discriminate on the grounds of faith. In any event, in all eight states the ban is applied specifically against Muslim women who wear the headscarf. In practical effect, the ban also discriminated on the grounds of gender. The measure effectively forces women to choose between their employment and the manifestation of their religious beliefs, violating their right to freedom of religion and equal treatment.[109]

Attempts to outlaw the *hijab* in German schools were initiated in October 2003 when seven regional states indicated their support for the view that the *hijab* should be banned from state schools. The discussions pertained both to students and teachers. In a highly publicised case in September that year, the highest judicial authority in the country, the federal Constitutional Court, ruled in favour of a Muslim teacher who had earlier been dismissed from her job for wearing the headscarf to school. The state of Baden-Württemberg had argued that a teacher with a headscarf violated "the strict neutrality of public schools in religious issues"[110].

However, the Court overturned this ruling declaring that states should strive for 'arrangements acceptable for everyone' in striking a balance between religious freedom and neutrality in schools. Nevertheless, the Court stated that states could take actions to prevent undue influence on children, but that the matter was too contentious to be decided on an ad hoc basis.

However, a new precedent was set in the state of Baden-Wurttemberg on 29 July 2008, when the State Administrative Court of Appeal in the city of Manheim ruled that teachers cannot cover their heads in the classrooms for religious reasons and as such, it upheld a ban on Muslim teachers wearing headscarves in the state. This effectively overturned a 2006 ruling of a lower court which had decided in favour of a teacher, Doris Graber, who had worn the headscarf since 1995. In justifying the latest decision, the Court claimed that a teacher's headscarf broke her obligation to keep religious expression out of the classroom[111].

It is interesting to note that Doris Graber had taught in the school wearing her *hijab* for thirteen years before the school board ordered her to stop covering her head in 2004. The timing of the schools' sudden change of perspective coincides with the ban of the *hijab* for Muslim students in neighbouring France the same year.

In many ways, the principle of strict neutrality in state affairs has shaped the discourse on the issue of the Muslim veil in Germany and to this extent, the arguments echo the French debates. On the other hand, unlike France, the German arguments presented in defence of such legislation are generally focused on the Christian nature of the country and feminist perspectives which associate the veil with women's oppression. State government officials like Annette Schavan (Regional Culture Minister) have openly justified this, stating that the state constitution placed Christian and western values and culture at the heart of the education system[112]. Resonant of a prevalent feminist perspective, she has further stated that the headscarf is "seen as a symbol of cultural division and part of a history of oppression of women."[113]

These laws appear to have been formulated to apply only to the headscarf or the Sikh turban while exempting Christian dress codes. Lawmakers in most states have been able to avoid allegations of discrimination by declaring the nun's habit occupational rather than religious. The only exception to this is found in the October 2004 judgment of the Federal Administrative Court which ruled that the state of Baden-Wuerttemburg's decision to ban the *hijab* was unlawful as it targeted one faith only. Consequently, nuns teaching in state schools now have to remove their habits before entering the classroom[114].

President Joahnnes Rau, however, opposed the discriminatory nature of these laws:

…State schools must respect each and everyone, whether Christian or pagan, agnostic, Muslim or Jew.… If the headscarf is an expression of religious faith, a dress with a missionary character, then that should apply equally to a monk's habit or a crucifix.[115]

He received a swift rebuttal from then state Prime Minister of Bavaria, Edmund Stoiber, and head of the Christian Social Union:

[The President has no right to] cast doubt on our national identity, distinguished by the Christian religion.

He described headscarves as a "political symbol incompatible with our democracy." (Ansari & Karim: 2004, p.5).

Thus, the discourse in Germany resonates with the heated exchanges over the issue in France in so far as the headscarf (and more recently, the *niqab* and *burqa*) are seen as a symbol of division separating Muslims from the host/wider society. In its February 2009 report, Human Rights Watch (HRW) documented a number of court cases brought to the European Court of Human Rights by non-Christians wishing to wear specific types of clothing for religious reasons in public office or schools in many of these German states. HRW condemned the European Court for its lack of sensitivity to minority rights and religious freedom in its approach to these cases. It highlighted the case of two twelve year old girls who were expelled from school in 1999 for refusing to remove their headscarves during physical education class. Their parents' suggestion to replace the headscarf with hats was rejected by the schools. However, the European Court upheld the school's decision and did not view it as a violation of the right to freedom of religion. It ruled that the girls had made an 'ostentatious' display of religion, even though the issue was actually whether a headscarf or hat is incompatible with physical education lessons. Its judgement was that the expulsions were not a disproportionate reaction, because the girls could continue their education by correspondence course.

Comparing such rulings with claims of religious discrimination raised by Christian complainants appealing to the Court, Human Rights Watch found that,

…when it comes to Muslim or Sikh manifestation of belief through particular clothes, the Court has been prepared to accept the denial of education to girls and women, or the denial of essential documents such as driving licenses.

Disappointed by the stance of the European Court of Human Rights on this issue, Human Rights Watch emphasises that these bans contradict Germany's international obligations to guarantee individuals' right to religious freedom and equality before the law. The rights watchdog believes that these laws (either explicitly or in their enforcement) effectively discriminate against Muslim women, and exclude them from teaching and other public sector jobs on the basis of their religion.

7.4 Sweden

Like France, Sweden prohibits the collection of data about its citizen's religious affiliation. In the absence of official statistics, various sources estimate the Muslim population at between 250,000 to 400,000, representing 1.8% to 4.4% of the country's total population of 9 million people[116]. The vast majority of the Muslim population is concentrated in the three urban centres of Stockholm, Goteborg and Malmo.

Various ethnicities are represented in the Swedish Muslim population including immigrants from Turkey, Iran, the Balkans, the Middle East, Somalia, Morocco and Pakistan. Like Britain, while in earlier decades Swedish Muslims primarily engaged in community activism and politics on the basis of shared ethnicity or cultural heritage, the second generation is evidently organising around a common Muslim identity. Unlike France and Germany, Sweden's approach to integration is more favourable to upholding its Muslim minority's rights. This became more apparent when, in 1997, the Government changed its 'immigration policy' to an 'integration policy' which aims to facilitate a dual process of changing the attitudes of both the host society and immigrants. This approach, which from the outset, seeks to share the responsibility of integration, is very different from the policies of France and Germany where the burden of assimilation rests squarely on the shoulders of immigrants. However, unlike Britain, its policy is not to be confused with multiculturalism. Sweden's integration policy does not differentiate between faith groups, ethnicity, gender or sexual orientation, but simply aims to promote equal rights, responsibilities and opportunities for all, based on diversity, mutual respect and tolerance.

This does not of course mean that there are no problems facing the Muslim minority. Indeed, the Muslim community in Sweden has been impacted by increasingly negative media coverage since 9/11. Some Swedes view Islam as incompatible with Swedish values. According to a 2007 Open Society Institute report, 'Muslims in the

EU: Sweden', there is only limited public acceptance of Muslim women wearing the *hijab*, or other types of veil, in public.

The wearing of the *hijab* has come under discussion in Sweden, although the government has not restricted its use. However, the state has allowed schools to regulate dress which covers the face of students. There are, therefore, parallels with the debate in the UK.

The Board of Integration's 2005 report acknowledges public perceptions towards veiling:

> The strongest support for wearing a headscarf is in public places [in the street] where almost a quarter is entirely or partly positive, whereas the weakest support applies to ID cards, where only 12% on the whole are entirely or partly positive. A general tendency in 2004 and 2005 is that those who are against the wearing of scarves are in the majority. However, the numbers of those who are entirely positive and those who decline to express an opinion are on the increase.

In recent years, the impact of veiling practices on Muslim women's access to education and the labour market has been illustrated by some legal cases.

The debates around these practices in schools in Sweden echo the arguments heard in Britain. While the *hijab* is widely seen as an expression of religion and hence non-negotiable, schools are allowed to ban full-face veils (like *niqabs* and *burqas*) on the basis that they hinder communication (and learning) in the classroom.

In spring 2006, the Swedish National Agency for Education upheld the right of a Muslim girl in the Minerva School (a non-denominational private school in the southern town of Umea) to wear the headscarf. The Minerva School, on the other hand, banned all kinds of headgear in the classroom (not just the *hijab*) and questioned its status as a religious observance. Its stance was that it is incorrect to suggest that a ban on veils prevents students from practicing their religion, given that there are many women who practice Islam yet do not cover their head.

In January 2007, when asked by the school to reconsider its ruling, the Agency reiterated its defence of pupils' rights to wear religious headgear in schools. It was concerned that a ban on all forms of headgear would lead to the exclusion of female students who wear headscarves for religious reasons. Commenting on the ruling, Frida Ericmats from the Agency said:

> We took another look at our first decision and found that there was nothing wrong there. It complied with both Swedish and international law…But freedom of religion is a constitutional right. [117]

She also pointed out that headscarves should not be equated with *burqas*. She said that the right to wear unobtrusive religious headgear is non-negotiable.

A similar victory was enjoyed by another Muslim girl in December 2008, a student of a secondary school in Landskrona in southern Sweden where she was studying a catering course. When the course's associated hotel refused to accept her as a trainee and the school subsequently advised her to remove headscarf, she decided to complain to the Ombudsman against Discrimination. The Ombudsman against Discrimination ruled in her favour and she was awarded 100,000 Kroner (equivalent to $7,400) as compensation. Since then, the school admitted that its actions were mistaken, while the hotel changed its regulations to allow students trying to gain work experience to wear any form of headscarf.[118]

Similarly, a number of cases have been reported in the media about Muslim women being denied jobs and occupational training due to their headscarf. In a prominent case in 2002, Nadia Gabriel, a Swedish woman of Palestinian origin, was selected to host a program on multiculturalism on Swedish public TV. The administration of the television channel blocked her appointment because of her headscarf. However, in an official decision in August 2003, the Swedish TV overturned this by declaring that Sweden respects cultures and religions and that religious freedom is guaranteed to all under the Swedish law. With this move, the Swedish TV became the first mainstream western television channel to allow a Muslim veiled woman to be a presenter.[119]

In 2006, a young Muslim girl was denied a job in an amusement park in Goteborg because she was wearing a *hijab*. She contested this in a court of law and won the case due to a combination of successful debate and media attention and was eventually offered the job.

Thus Muslim women in Sweden appear to have greater options in exercising the right to wear a veil (albeit limited to the headscarf) in the public sphere.

7.5 Turkey

Turkey is the latest and only Muslim-majority country to apply for full membership of the European Union (in 2005). As the census does not ask people to declare their religious belief, there are no accurate statistics available to gauge the number of Muslims in Turkey. However, there are various sources which claim that according to the Government of Turkey, 99.8% of the country's 71 million people are Muslim. Turkey is a secular republic with no official state religion, though its Constitution respects freedom of religions. Turkey's uniqueness for the purposes of this analysis lies in the fact that it is the only Muslim-majority European country to ban the headscarf in universities. However, despite the ban, an estimated 62% of Muslim women in Turkey wear the headscarf according to the Turkish Economic and Social Studies Foundation[120]. The year 2008 saw massive street protests against attempts by the Government to overturn this ban. Indeed, the headscarf row in Turkey has come to symbolise the very tensions of her complex socio-political map. It is a very emotional issue and symbolises the power struggle between a rising, increasingly wealthy middle class of religious Turks and the secular élite, backed by the military and the judiciary.

"In Turkey, the turban [as the traditional male headscarf is known] has always been an issue of 'backwardness' against 'modernity', explains Ayse Kadioglu, a professor at the Political Science Department at the Sabanci University. (This dates back to Attatürk's ban of traditional headgears in the 1920s.)

Twenty years ago, Turkish authorities imposed the ban on the headscarf (known in Turkey as the turban) in universities and colleges and government institutions claiming that the growing number of covered women in campuses threatened secularism – one of the founding principles of present-day Turkey. At that time, there were very few headscarves visible on the streets of Turkey. However, today, surveys show that over 60% of women in Turkey wear a headscarf.

Rights activist Sanar Yurdatapan is not convinced. "We don't want to be an Algeria or an Iran, a country where women are forced to wear head coverings", she told The Chicago Tribune. "But what is the difference between forcing someone to wear something or requiring them to take it off? The human rights are the same."

In February 2008, Turkish lawmakers voted to change the Constitution in a way that would guarantee all citizens the right to go to college irrespective of their dress. The secular opposition in the country voted against the measure but lost the motion. Nevertheless, thousands gathered in street protests to lodge their anger at the move which they felt undermined secularism and Turkish women's ability to resist being forced to veil by family or religious authorities.

Secularists and feminists feared that once the headscarf is allowed on campus, it will make its way into the civil service and eventually become a source of religious and social pressure on millions of women who do not cover up.

On 5 June 2008, this law was overturned by Turkey's constitutional court, dominated by secularists, who revered the changes made earlier in the year relaxing restrictions on the wearing of the headscarf. The court ruled that allowing the scarf to be worn on campus and in government buildings infringed on the secularist principles of the constitution. This argument has strong similarities with those heard in France and Germany.

After examining the contexts of Ireland, France, Germany and Sweden, it seems that the debate over the Muslim veil depends much on the underlying policy of integration implemented in a given country. In France and Germany, the principles of secularism and state neutrality are so strongly entrenched that, coupled with the policy of assimilation, they leave little space for veiled women to comfortably participate as fully-fledged members of society. In Sweden and Ireland, where the policy of integration respects diversity without demanding conformity to the host society's values or culture, Muslim women are able to enjoy more freedom to choose their dress codes. Turkey's case reveals the diversity of opinion in a Muslim-majority country and that banning the veil does not necessarily lead to the eradication of the practice of veiling. Many claim that banning the veil has the adverse impact of excluding women from education and participation in the labour force, while others argue that it removes peer pressure to veil.

It is interesting to note that while most of the arguments on banning Muslim women's dress codes have centred on claims of secularism and the notion that veils impede Muslim minority citizens integration in wider society, no such concern has been demonstrated for the integration of Muslim men who also visibly practice Muslim dress codes in the form of growing beards and wearing traditional Middle Eastern garments (especially out of office or while attending religious gatherings). Could it be that this is because beards are more familiar to Europe than the veil?

It is difficult to imagine the UK heading the way of France or Germany in banning the Muslim veil from schools or public sector institutions. Perhaps this is one benefit of Britain's policy of multiculturalism which calls for mutual respect and defends the rights of faith communities without demanding submission to 'British culture'. What British culture really is, what 'British values' are and what it means to be 'British' have been the subject of many articles in the media over the past few years. Moreover, for now, the strength of organised Muslim community activism and its ties with the Labour Party, means the community is able to stand up to any right-wing pressure for calls to ban any form of veiling in the UK. This is not to say that restrictions on dress codes are only an expression of right-wing viewpoints, racism or Islamophobia. Indeed, there are several well-supported reasons why many women, Muslim and non-Muslim, publicly oppose veiling. One lesson that can be drawn from this comparative analysis, is the recognition that any form of official policy or legislation which seeks to either condemn or endorse veiling, will inevitably cause more harm than good. Instead, what is needed is discussion and dialogue that create more understanding between both camps and do not demand or campaign for any type of state regulation. After all, this is a matter of dress.

Chapter 8: Conclusion

This research has sought to take stock of the current debates on the veil in Britain, by: mapping key challenges facing British Muslim women posed by their community and wider society, and the strategies employed by them to cope with intersecting forms of discrimination. Some have adopted the veil as a powerful tool to escape traditional gender roles and assert their identity against racism and xenophobia, sexism and patriarchal rules. My respondents fiercely defended their right to wear the veil as an expression of their freedom of choice.

The fact that politico-religious groups may be sponsoring the importation and spread of these dress codes to Britain (and indeed other western countries with Muslim populations) does not necessarily mean women allow themselves to be used by these fundamentalist groups, nor does it mean that they endorse all that these groups stand for. On the contrary, veiled British Muslim women are often active agents in using these ideologies to their own advantage and to promote them for their own interests.

India Knight's article in The Times, 'Muslims are the new Jews' published on 15 October 2006, accurately summarises British Muslim women's fury and reaction to Jack Straw's opposition to the full-face veil and the current heated debate on the veil in Britain.

> It has become acceptable to say the most ignorant, degrading things about Islam. And then we all sit around wondering why young Muslim men appear to be getting angrier and more politicised, or why 'westernised' young Muslim women whose mothers go bare-headed are suddenly, defiantly, opting for the full-on *niqab*-style veil that leaves only a slit for the eyes.

> I am particularly irked by ancient old 'feminists' wheeling out themselves and their 30-years-out-of-date opinions to reiterate the old chestnut that Islam, by its nature, oppresses women (unlike the Bible, eh?) and that the veil compounds the blanket oppression.

> In their view, all Muslim women are crushed because they can't wear visible lipstick or flash their thongs. Does it occur to these idiots... that perhaps there exist large sections of our democratic society, veiled or otherwise, who have every right to their modesty, just as their detractors have every right to wear push-up bras?[121]

What was common to all the research participants was the need for a new identity, as Muslims and the veil embodied this sense of solidarity. The extent to which the veil is a successful strategy depends not only on the benefits of this appeal in the short term, but also its social and political ramifications on the community as a whole, in the long run. It is clear from the debate that British society, in large parts, is not ready to accept dress codes, deemed Muslim, beyond the headscarf, in their educational institutions or private companies. When confronted with such messages, women who continue to veil, will inevitably find themselves further alienated in society. The impact of this alienation will not be restricted to their status as women alone, as they are denied employment and educational opportunities. Such isolation and the circle of resentment it will create, will force the community to live in an isolated, parallel world with separate institutions limiting the scope for the delicate balance of the existing multicultural set-up.

Such a scenario is extremely worrying and should be a priority for opinion makers and government leaders to avoid. A greater understanding needs to be built around the motivations for Muslim women's adoption of the veil and some of the major issues of racism, religious discrimination and gender discrimination intertwined with it. While the piece of cloth covering British Muslim women's heads has been under the magnifying glass for some years now, perhaps it is time to scrutinise the wider society's perceptions and attitudes towards the veil. What is it that makes non-Muslim British people wary of the veil? Is their condemnation based on an altruistic, even if patronising, desire to 'free Muslim women from oppression'? Or is it simply that the veil is so unfamiliar that it is deemed incompatible with 'British values'?

Irrespective of the motivations of veiling, what the wider society fails to realise is that by failing to engage with veiled women, it is denying the agency which these women exercise in their private and public lives. They miss the reality that for many British Muslim women, *hijab* is a passport for engaging with society. As the Local Government Secretary Hazel Blears observed at a meeting with Muslim community members in Birmingham in January 2008:

> Public debate about Muslim women too often reverts to stereotypes and preconceptions. We pay too much attention to Muslim women's appearance – with the perennial debate about headscarves and veils – and too little to what they say and do.[122]

The risks of not engaging with veiled women and continuing to regard them with hostility and prejudice are high, as they will only swell the ranks of fundamentalist forces (and not just by some veiled women). This will lead to an even more polarised and divided society.

Britain's case illustrates that it is time to re-evaluate our framework of assessing women's empowerment in Muslim contexts – including in the diaspora – and to use alternative frameworks of power and agency to understand the lives of women from Muslim communities and the challenges they confront. Policies that force women to wear the veil in the name of religion are as damaging to women's rights as those which prohibit women from wearing the veil in the name of preserving secularism and neutrality. In both cases, the effect is the same: women's options are limited rather than increased; their access to education curtailed; their participation in the job market impeded and the goal of social cohesion becomes further out of reach. Both types of regulation, which can be considered as two extremes, undermine women's individual autonomy, choice, agency and self-expression.

At the same time, in so far as the veil is a visible marker of identity, the longer-term implication of asserting this identity on the basis of religion seems to suggest a steady erosion of wider alliances with secular groups, feminists and anti-racism campaigners. As the new generation of British Muslim women activists seems to assert its identity on the basis of religious affiliation, it is losing wider links of solidarity with women's rights groups and other civil society pressure groups. Being rewarded for forming such narrow groups in the name of diversity, is surely not good news for social cohesion. The risk of isolation is as great as the risk of creating rivalry, bitterness and resentment as Britain's 'faith communities' compete for state funding and concessions. As we continue to negotiate our way through multiculturalism, do we really want to live in a world fragmented by identity politics? It is time that the official patronage of faith-based groups and the policy of engaging with British Muslim women on the basis of their faith is re-examined for it is leading to a path of divided communities rather than social cohesion.

The British brand of multiculturalism seems to be creating divisiveness by enabling different treatment on the basis of the right to difference, rather than facilitating the right to 'equal treatment despite difference'. This does not bode well for the rights of British Muslim women in areas where multiculturalism, and the associated state patronage of traditional, often hard-line groups, (dominated by men claiming to represent the interests of British Muslims, serves to silence women. It means that when British Muslim women are faced with attempts to curtail their freedom and rights in the name of religion, justified by community leaders under the banner of multiculturalism, they often self-censor for fear of tarnishing the image of their 'community'. There are few British Muslim women activists – veiled and unveiled – who are trying to challenge this predominantly male community leadership and represent their own interests. However, it is crucial that they critically evaluate the prevailing understanding of multiculturalism and do not end up becoming state-sponsored agents of change. Equally, they need to appreciate the importance of transcending religious boundaries and establishing links with broader coalitions in order to avoid isolation. Otherwise, while they would have successfully freed themselves of the dominance of their own male community leadership, the parameters of their struggle will have reinforced divided communities. In other words, they would have won only one battle by voluntarily excluding themselves from the mainstream.

Perhaps more questions have been raised in this book than answered and it is hoped that these serve as a basis for future academic enquiry. Undertaking such work places a great responsibility on the researcher to provide an informed analysis with sensitivity without comprising the position of British Muslim women either in their own community or the wider society. It is almost as tight a rope to walk on for the researcher, as it is for the subject.

Endnotes

1 Jack Straw is a very senior Labour Party politician who served as the Leader of the House of Commons from 2006 to 2007.

2 Jack Straw, "I felt uneasy talking to someone I couldn't see", *The Guardian*, October 6, 2006, http://politics.guardian.co.uk/labour/story/0,,1888847,00.html#article_continue. The article was first published in a local paper in Lancashire (Jack Straw's constituency) known as the Evening Telegraph.

3 This position was held by Philip James Woolas from May 2005 to June 2007, a Labour Party MP.

4 Since Jack Straw's use of the term 'full veil' in his article to refer to a headscarf which covers either the whole face with or without a narrow slit for the eyes, the term is widely used in the media interchangeably with 'full-face veil', *niqab* and *burqa*. *Burqa*, an Urdu term, is an outer garment consisting of a loose coat-like full length gown and a separate headgear of the same material to cover the head (face and hair). It is traditionally worn by women in India and Pakistan.

5 In his article (refer to footnote 2), Jack Straw wrote that the full veil was "such a visible statement of separation and of difference." Two weeks later, in a televised interview with the BBC, Prime Minister Tony Blair echoed similar sentiments saying that "It is a mark of separation and that is why it makes other people from outside the community feel uncomfortable." (Blair's concerns over face veils, BBC, October 17, 2006).

6 Harriet Ruth Harman is an important Labour politician. Since June 2007, she has been the Deputy Leader and Party Chair of the Labour Party. On 28 June 2007, she was appointed Leader of the House of Commons, Lord Privy Seal and Minister for Women and Equality. On 12 October 2007, she became head of a new UK Government Department, the Government Equalities Office. Her comment quoted above was reported in: "Veil harms equal right - Harman," *BBC News*, October 11, 2006, http://news.bbc.co.uk/1/hi/uk_politics/6040016.stm

7 Helm, Toby, "Back British values or lose grants, Kelly tells Muslim groups," *Telegraph*, October 12, 2006, http://www.telegraph.co.uk/news/uknews/1531226/Back-British-values-or-lose-grants,-Kelly-tells-Muslim-groups. html

8 WEMC is an abbreviation for the 'Women's Empowerment in Muslim Contexts' project set up in April 2005. This Research Programme Consortium comprises eight partners in four countries, China, Indonesia, Iran and Pakistan. More information about the project is available on the WEMC website at: http://www.wemc.com.hk

9 The gradual downfall of the trade union movement and anti-racist organizations has culminated in the development of many religious and Islamic organizations among the Muslim community who themselves are from many different ethnic backgrounds.

10 The Tablighi Jama'at is a Sunni, reformist movement which was initiated by Maulana Ilyas in 1926 in Mewat, northern India. Literally translated from Urdu as the 'assembly of preachers', the network works at the very grassroots level to preach Islam by following the example of the Prophet Muhammad (PBUH) and the Qur'an. Today, it has evolved into a transnational movement active in India, Pakistan, Bangladesh, the UK and several other countries. The founder's six principles of preaching are: i) believing in the oneness of Allah, ii) offering the five prayers daily, iii) gaining knowledge and the remembrance of Allah, iv) respecting every Muslim, v) honesty and sincerity of intention and vi) spare time for travelling for this work. The modus operandi of the preaching involves personal service and sacrifice by dispatching groups of self-funded volunteers who spare their resources and time to visit select communities for the purposes preaching. The length of these preaching missions varies between 3 days and 40 days. Ideologically, the Tablighi Jama'at has *Deobandi* leanings. Some observers have also sought to uncover linkages between the Jama'at and *Wahhabism* promoted by Saudi Arabia, and indications of Saudi Arabian-funded groups subsidising some of the mosques built by the movement and the travel of the volunteer missionaries. It is organised as a loose network with the international headquarters, the Nizamuddin Markaz, based in Delhi, India. There is a culture of holding annual congregations of members with the largest held in Tongi, Bangladesh. The second largest is held in Raiwind, on the outskirts of Lahore in Pakistan. In the UK, the group's activities are coordinated by the Dewsbury Markaz in West Yorkshire. It claims to be a non-political, non-violent missionary movement and refrains from making any political statements publicly. Since 9/11, the Tablighi Jama'at has come under scrutiny by British intelligence and security forces after some suspects of 7 July 2005, London bombing were said to have attended the Dewsbury Markaz.

11 The 'Al-Huda International Welfare Foundation' was set up by an Islamic scholar, Dr. Farhat Hashmi, in 1994 in Pakistan. Today, it has a branch in Canada as well. The objectives of Al-Huda, as proclaimed on their website, is to "promote purely Islamic values and thinking based on sound knowledge and research" and to work for the welfare of the 'deprived classes'. The Foundation offers various types of structured courses particularly for women and girls to gain religious education including online courses. Additionally, it has an outreach programme aimed at women and girls in prisons, hospitals and rural areas. Al-Huda insists that it is a non-political, non-sectarian NGO. Dr. Farhat Hashmi seems to be leading a missionary movement to educate women and girls about 'Islamic principles' and how these can be applicable to their daily lives. She runs the Foundation with her husband, also a religious scholar. They claim to have "dedicated their lives to eradicate as much as possible, ignorance, increasing materialism and spiritual deprivation

from society by spreading the light of the Qur'an". Many secular Pakistanis and feminists believe that Al-Huda is propagating a puritanical interpretation of Islam commonly known as *Wahhabism*. More details about the organisation can be accessed at Al-Huda's website: http://www.alhudapk.com//home/about-us

12   Established in November 1997, the Muslim Council of Britain (MCB) is the largest umbrella organisation of 350 institutions affiliated to it including mosques, education and charitable institutions, women and youth organisations and professional bodies. It is widely consulted by the British Government on matters pertaining to the Muslim community. MCB has so far been allied with the Labour Party. It has emerged as the focal leader of Muslim activism in Britain and has come to enjoy a privileged position of credibility in consultations and advocacy. Based in London, it has an elaborate organisational structure with the General Assembly comprised of delegates from affiliated bodies. The other organisational units within the MCB are a Central Working Committee (CWC), various specialist committees and task groups, and a Board of Counsellors. Of its seventeen specialist committees, women are represented in only four.

13   "Religion in Britain" Office for National Statistics, United Kingdom, 2001, http://www.statistics.gov.uk/cci/nugget. asp?id=293s
This is the first census which asked respondents to indicate their religious affiliation. Earlier census data of 1991 and 1983 only included questions of ethnic origin which made assessment of the number of British Muslims difficult and dependent on extrapolation from available information about the country of birth and origin. The inclusion of the religious affiliation data as well as ethnic origin in the census has been in response to persistent campaigns by the Muslim Council of Britain. However, it must be noted that in the 2001 census, the religion question was voluntary and 4,011,000 people chose not answer it (i.e. 7.7 %).

14   "Muslims in Europe: Country Guide", *BBC News*, December 23, 2005, http://news.bbc.co.uk/1/hi/world/europe/4385768.stm

15   Dobs, Joy, Hazel Green and Linda Zealey, eds, *Focus on Ethnicity and Religion*, National Statistics, 2006, 66, http://www.statistics.gov.uk/downloads/theme_compendia/foer2006/FoER_Main.pdf

16   Please refer to Daniele Joly, *Britannia's Crescent: Making a Place for Muslims in British Society*, Ashgate Publishing Ltd, United Kingdom, 1995.

17   See John Rex, "Islam in the United Kingdom in Islam, Europe's Second Religion," in *Islam, Europe's Second Religion*, ed. Shireen T. Hunter, Centre for Strategic and International Studies, 2002, 51 – 57.

18   'Canal colonies' is the term used for the settlements along the vast network of canal irrigation set up in the Punjab by the British in the late nineteenth century which turned large tracts of arid land into great centres of commercialised agriculture in South Asia.

19   Malik, K., "Born in Bradford", *Prospect*, October 2005, http://www.kenanmalik.com/essays/bradford_prospect.html

20   Gupta, Rahila, "An all-too familiar affair", *The Guardian*, February 21, 2009, http://www.guardian.co.uk/commentisfree/belief/2009/feb/20/rushdie-fatwa-religion

21   7/7 refers to the series of coordinated suicide attacks on London's public transport network on the morning of 7 July 2005. Three bombs exploded on three London Underground trains while a fourth was detonated on a bus during the morning rush hour. Fifty-six people were killed in these incidents (including the bombers) while another 700 were injured.

22   "Muslim women to advise Government on preventing violent extremism", Communities and Local Government Department website, November 21, 2007, http://www.communities.gov.uk/news/corporate/554064

23   In this context, the term 'progressive' is not used in its historical sense of indicating a left-of-centre position in politics which favours state intervention. Rather, it is simply used in its literal sense to imply a willingness to improve, change and progress towards better conditions by advocating more enlightened and liberal ideas. The author acknowledges that the description of 'progressive' varies according to people's normative judgments, frameworks and beliefs.

24   "Muslim Groups Patronising", *Asian Image*, October 27, 2008, http://www.asianimage.co.uk/uk/3796060.Muslim_groups_patronising_/

25   Beckfordm, Martin, "Baroness Warsi: Labour's Young Muslim Advisory Group is Patronising and Divisive", *Telegraph*, October 7, 2008, http://www.telegraph.co.uk/news/newstopics/politics/labour/3155177/Baroness-Warsi-Labours-Young-Muslim-Advisory-Group-is-patronising-and-divisive.html

26   Glynn, Sarah, "Liberalising Islam: Creating Brits of the Islamic Persuasion," The University of Edinburgh, April 2008, http://www.geos.ed.ac.uk/homes/sglynn/Liberalising_Islam.pdf

27   MPACUK is a non-profit organisation which has emerged as a vocal advocacy group for the rights of British Muslim community. Established after the events of 9/11, it initially aimed to counter the negative perception of Muslims in the media but has since taken up other causes. It claims not to be a charity "but a unique Empowerment System; the first of its kind for Muslims in Europe". It aims to "defend Muslim interests and Islam throughout Britain and the world…. Tired of a government attitude of mere interest in using Muslim groups and individuals to support its policies, rather than taking account of the Muslim voice, MPACUK is aiming to politicise Muslims and encourage them to get to know their Members of Parliament, and to feel confident in raising issues with them – it is after all their job to look

after the interests of their constituents." (Source: MPACUK website: http://www.mpacuk.org/content/view/2046/98/)

28 "Women Only Jihad", Dispatches, by Tazeen Ahmad, *Channel 4*, October 30, 2006. http://video.google.co.uk/videoplay?docid=-3046570183637153703&q=dispatches

29 Department for Communities and Local Government, "Engaging with Muslim Women: A Report from the Prime Minister's Event", Communities and Local Government Publications, September 2006, http://www.womenandequalityunit.gov.uk/publications/muslimwomenfeedrep.pdf
This report is of the meeting hosted by the Prime Minister, Tony Blair and the Ministers for Women, Ruth Kelly and Meg Munn, at 10 Downing Street on 10 May 2006 where some 40 British Muslim women were invited for a special consultation and effort to hear Muslim women's perspectives on issues and challenges facing their community and steps to tackle extremism in the post 7/7 world.

30 This was reported by Fareena Alam, "My Battle is in the Living Room", *The Guardian*, March 30, 2003, http://observer.guardian.co.uk/islam/story/0,,925719,00.html

31 "Me and the Mosque", by Zarqa Nawas, National Film Board of Canada, 2005, 52 min 45 s, http://www.onf-nfb.gc.ca/fra/collection/film/?id=51517

32 This is the same 8,000 square metre London Muslim Centre which was built beside the East London Mosque in 2004 and which received funding from the borough council, the London Development Authority, the European Development Fund and the Government's Surestart Programme.

33 These views were expressed by trainers and participants at the Life Coaching Workshop (held on 26 April and 10 May 2008 at the Central Mosque of Brent (North London). The Workshop was organised by 'Live 4 U' in collaboration with the Women's Consortium (another grassroots Muslim community organisation based in the London Borough of Brent).

34 Website: http://www.thecitycircle.com/

35 Website: http://www.muslimprofessionals.org.uk

36 The website of 'Islamic Circles, Muslim Marriage Events' can be accessed at http://www.muslimmarriageevents.org/

37 Nazlee, Shazia, *The Hijab:Dress for Every Muslimah – An Encouragement and Clarification*, Jam 'iat Ihyaa' Minhaaj al-Sunnah, United Kingdom, 2005.

38 Obaidullah Almuslim, Muhammad, trans., *Adornment of Women in Forensic and Medical Perspective*, Vision Printing, Publishing & Distribution, Pakistan, 2002. This book was written by a Saudi Arabian author and later translated from Arabic to English by Muhammad Obaidullah Almuslim in Pakistan.

39 Alarcon, Abu Maryam Isma'eel, trans., *Three Essays on the Obligation of Veiling*, Al-Ibaanah Book Publishing, USA, 2003. The three essays were originally authored by three religious scholars from Saudi Arabia, in the twentieth century: Abdul-Azeez bin Abdillaah bin Baaz, Muhammad bin Salih Al-Uthaimeen and Zayd bin Haadee Al-Madkhalee.

40 Ibrahim, Yasmin, *I Can Wear My Hijab Anywhere!*, The Islamic Foundation, United Kingdom, 2004.

41 Such criticisms were also heard at the WLUML's UK Pre-Plan of Action Meeting on 30 June 2006 by various British Muslim academics and social activists, who referred for example to the United Nations' Convention on the Rights of the Child. This meeting was personally attended by the author.

42 S. I. Mogra, personal communication, August 17, 2006. Ibrahim Mogra is a British graduate imam in Leicester and chair of the Mosque and Community Affairs Committee of the Muslim Council of Britain.

43 Hijab Trials, http://www.islamchannel.tv/citysisters/HijabTrial.aspx (accessed August 1, 2008)

44 This was reported by the BBC on 29 November 2006 in "Survey finds support for veil ban" which highlighted the findings of an ICM survey based on the answers of some 1004 respondents. The survey found 56% opposed to a government ban on face-covering veils with nearly one in 10 saying they did not know. For further details, please visit: http://news.bbc.co.uk/1/hi/uk/6194032.stm

45 S. I. Mogra, personal communication, 17 August 2006.

46 Women Living Under Muslim Laws, *Plan of Action – Dhaka 1997*, (1999), 7 - 24.

47 This conversation occurred in the presence of the author at the Muslim Marriage Event at the Qur'anic Markaz Trust, South Woodford Muslim Community Centre on 13 April 2008. The event, advertised through community listings, was organised by Dr. Fahim and Nadia Bushra (a young Muslim activist) to provide a safe space for young Muslims to meet one another in an 'Islamic setting' to find prospective marriage partners. The Muslim Marriage Event takes place every month at the centre and is usually attended by some 100 young men and women from across the city and suburbs of London. The two-hour event starts with a lecture by Dr. Fahim on the rights and responsibilities of Muslims in marriage, followed by group work by participants where each group consists of three women and three men who are asked to discuss an issue related to marriage and then share their conclusions with the whole audience. On 13 April, the discussion topic was 'What is culture?' and in what ways this impacts the choice of spouse and marriage for British Muslims.

48 Association of Muslim Schools statistics:

http://www.ams-uk.org/index.php?option=com_content&task=view&id=13&Itemid=45 (accessed, March 6, 2007)

49 Apart from these five Muslim schools, there are 6,955 Christian, 36 Jewish and 2 Sikh schools bring the total figure of state funded faith schools to 7000 (including 600 secondary and 6,400 primary schools). Source: Taylor, M., "Two-Thirds Oppose State Aided Faith Schools", *The Guardian*, August 23, 2005 (see Bibliography for details).The total number of schools in England maintained by the state is 22,000 - Source: DfES, "Religious Education in Faith Schools", April 27, 2006, http://findoutmore.dfes.gov.uk/2006/02/religious_educa.html
According to the (latest) 2001 national census, the religious affiliation profile of the country shows Christians at 72% of the total population, followed by Muslims at nearly 3%, Hindus at 1%, Sikhs at 0.6%, Jews at 0.5%, Buddhists at 0.3%, and people from other religions at 0.3%. 15.5% claim not to follow any religion while 7.3% did not state any religion. Source: Census, April 2001,"Religion in the UK'", Office for National Statistics, February 13, 2003: http://www.statistics.gov.uk/cci/nugget.asp?id=293

50 The first National Framework for Religious Education was launched on 28 October 28 2004 by DfES. It endorses the entitlement to religious education for all students and provides a framework for high quality education of the basic tenets of Christianity, Judaism, Hinduism, Sikhism, Buddhism and Islam. However, the Framework is non-statutory and while many faith schools do teach some aspects of other faiths, there is no legal requirement for them to do so.

51 This was established by a survey conducted for The Guardian newspaper by ICM who interviewed a random sample of 1,006 adults aged 18+ by telephone between 12 and 14 August 2005 – after 7 July 2005 terrorist bombings in London. Interviews were conducted across the country and the results have been weighted to the profile of all adults. Taylor, Matthew, "Two-Thirds Oppose State Aided Faith Schools", *The Guardian*, August 23, 2005, http://education.guardian.co.uk/faithschools/story/0,13882,1554593,00.html

52 Matthew Taylor, "Two-Thirds Oppose State Aided Faith Schools", *The Guardian*, August 23, 2005, http://education.guardian.co.uk/faithschools/story/0,13882,1554593,00.html

53 This book adopts WLUML's definition of the word 'fundamentalism': the use of religion (and, often, ethnicity and culture) to gain and mobilize political power. WLUML, *Plan of Action – Dhaka 1997*, United Kingdom, 1999, http://www.wluml.org/node/451

54 This concern for poor quality has also been highlighted in Polly Curtis, "Teachers Lack Faith in Muslim Schools", *The Guardian*, June 9, 2004 http://education.guardian.co.uk/faithschools/story/0,,1234836,00.html

55 Sahgal, Gita and Nira Yuval-Davis, ed., *Refusing Holy Orders: Women and Fundamentalism in Britain*, WLUML, United Kingdom, 2000

56 Sahgal, Gita and Nira Yuval-Devis, "Introduction: Fundamentalism, Multiculturalism and Women in Britain." In *Refusing Holy Orders, Women and Fundamentalism in Britain*, WLUML, United Kingdom, 2000, 7-31.

57 Versi, Ahmed J, "Giving Muslims a Voice", *Muslim Council of Britain*, August 18, 2004, http://www.mcb.org.uk/features/feature_print.php?ann_id=442

58 The Children's Legal Centre is an independent national charity concerned with law and policy affecting children and young people.

59 "Schoolgirl Loses Muslim Gown Case", *BBC News*, June 15, 2004, http://news.bbc.co.uk/1/hi/education/3808073.stm

60 "Siddiqui welcomes High Court judgment on Jilbab controversy", The Muslim Parliament of Great Britain, June 15, 2004, http://www.muslimparliament.org.uk/Jilbab.htm

61 This was obtained from The Children's Legal Centre's website: "Landmark Victory in Muslim Dress Case", http://www.childrenslegalcentre.com/Templates/Internal.asp?NodeID=90845

62 "Schoolgirl Wins Muslim Gown Case", *BBC News*, March 2, 2005, http://news.bbc.co.uk/1/hi/england/beds/bucks/herts/4310545.stm

63 John, Cindi and Dominic Casciani, "Muslim Modesty in the Spotlight", *BBC News*, March 3, 2005, http://news.bbc.co.uk/go/pr/fr/-/1/hi/uk/4315839.stm

64 "Schoolgirl Wins Muslim Gown Case", *BBC News*, March 2, 2005, http://news.bbc.co.uk/1/hi/england/beds/bucks/herts/4310545.stm

65 "School Wins Muslim Dress Appeal", *BBC News*, March 22, 2006, http://news.bbc.co.uk/go/pr/fr/-/1hi/education/4832072.stm

66 "School Wins Muslim Dress Appeal", *BBC News*, March 22, 2006, http://news.bbc.co.uk/go/pr/fr/-/1hi/education/4832072.stm

67 Johnson, Boris, "The Shabina Begum Case Never Had Anything to do With Modesty", *Telegraph*, March 23,2006, http://www.telegraph.co.uk/opinion/main.jhtml?xml=/opinion/2006/03/23/do2303.xml&sSheet=/news/2006/03/23/ixnewstop.html

68 "School Wins Muslim Dress Appeal", *BBC News*, March 22, 2006,

http://news.bbc.co.uk/go/pr/fr/-/1hi/education/4832072.stm

69   "Schoolgirl speaks out on win", *BBC News (video)*, March 2, 2005,
     http://news.bbc.co.uk/player/nol/newsid_4310000/newsid_4311000/4311069.
     stm?bw=nb&mp=rm&news=1&ms3=0&ms_javascript=true&bbcws=2

70   Gerard, Jasper J., "Gerard Meets Shabina Begum: Faith, the Veil, Shopping and Me", *Sunday Times*, March 26, 2006,
     http://www.timesonline.co.uk/tol/news/article696181

71   Mendick, Robert and Kiran Randhawa, "Muslim Girl's Brother Linked to Islam Radicals", *London Evening Standard*,
     March 4, 2005,
     http://www.thisislondon.co.uk/news/article-17038092-details/Muslim+girl%27s+brother+linked+to+Islam+radicals/
     article.do

72   "Schools Allowed to Ban Face-Veils", *BBC News*, March 20, 2007,
     http://news.bbc.co.uk/go/pr/fr/-/1hi/education/6466221.stm

73   Hall, Macer, "At Last The Veil Banned in Class", *Daily Express*, May 7, 2007, http://www.express.co.uk/posts/view/6377

74   Press Association, "Veil Row Teacher Sacked", *The Guardian*, November 24, 2006,
     http://www.guardian.co.uk/education/2006/nov/24/schools.uk

75   Norfolk, Andrew, "Dewsbury: Kidnapping, Lynching and a Suicide", *Times Online*, May 28, 2008,
     http://www.timesonline.co.uk/tol/news/uk/crime/article4016574.ece

76   Alam, Fareeha, "We Must Move Beyond the Hijab", *The Guardian*, November 29, 2005,
     http://education.guardian.co.uk/higher/news/story/0,,1653211,00.html

77   "MECO supports Niqab Ban in Schools", MECO, February 5, 2007,
     http://www.meco.org.uk/press18.htm

78   Such as: Lindley, J., A. Dale and S. Dex, *Ethnic Differences in Women's Demographic, Family Characteristics and Economic
     Activity Profiles, 1992-2002*, Labour Market Trends, April 2004.

79   Botcherby, S., "Moving On Up? Ethnic Minority Women at Work", Equal Opportunities Commission, United
     Kingdom, September 2006.

80   Ahmed, Samira, "Women Slipping Thru' The Gaps", *Q News*, March 2005, 13. Q News is a popular Muslim community
     magazine published monthly in the UK.

81   For instance, while 65% of black Caribbean women work full-time, just 14% of Pakistani and 27% of Bangladeshi
     women do.

82   "Higher Education Institutions Obstacles to Muslim Women", the *Muslim News*, August 25, 2006.

83   Smith, Laura, "My Manager Said I Looked Like a Terrorist", *The Guardian*, September 7, 2006,
     http://www.guardian.co.uk/print/0,,329570618-103680,00.html

84   Quoted in Laura Smith, "My Manager Said I Looked Like a Terrorist", *The Guardian*, September 7, 2006,
     http://www.guardian.co.uk/print/0,,329570618-103680,00.html

85   Dr. David Tyrer of Liverpol John Moores University and Fauzia Ahmad of the University of Bristol jointly conducted
     this research into Muslim women and higher education to explore the challenges faced by Muslim women in accessing
     higher education and strategies to overcome these obstacles. The study was based on interviews of 93 Muslim women
     between the ages of 19 and 26.

86   Special Correspondent, "Higher Education Institutions Obstacles to Muslim Women", the *Muslim News*, August 25,
     2006, 10, http://higher-education-news.newslib.com/story/217-3242437/

87   Department for Communities and Local Government, "Engaging with Muslim Women: A Report from the Prime
     Minister's Event", Communication and Local Government Publications, September 2006,
     http://www.womenandequalityunit.gov.uk/publications/muslimwomenfeedrep.pdf

88   With Muslims making up to one million of seven million Londoners, there should be around 3,000 Muslim police
     officers rather than the 100 or so in force at the time.

89   This was revealed in a press statement by the then Association of Muslim Police chairman, Inspector Richard Varley.

90   NHS is the country's National Health Service.

91   Triggle, Nick, "Dress Code Deters Muslim Medics", *BBC News*, June 29, 2006,
     http://news.bbc.co.uk/go/pr/fr/-/1/hi/health/4634351.stm

92   The *Muslim News*, established in 1989, is the most widely read Muslim community newspaper in the UK. It's a monthly
     publication which can be accessed on the internet as well at: http://www.muslimnews.co.uk

93   "Islamic Games Give British Women the Option", the *Muslim News*, September 21, 2005,
     http://www.muslimnews.co.uk/news.php?article=9902

94   Robinson, Nina, "Muslims 'Face Barriers' Over Sport", *BBC News*, August 25, 2006,

http://news.bbc.co.uk/go/pr/fr/-/1/hi/uk/5286568.stm

95 "Minister, Mayor Backs British Muslim Football Team", the *Muslim News*, September 16, 2005, http://www.muslimnews.co.uk/index/press.php?pr=214

96 Bee, Peta, "Running Under Cover", *The Guardian*, November 20, 2007, http://www.guardian.co.uk/uk/2007/nov/20/race.healthandwellbeing.html

97 Wajid, Sara, "Enter the Ninjah: More Muslim Women Take up Martial Arts in Britain", *Gulf Times*, June 21, 2007, http://www.gulf-times.com/mritems/streams/2007/6/20/2_156296_1_255.pdf

98 The IHRC is a UK-based independent rights organisation seeking to protect the rights of Muslims and promoting equality, racial harmony etc.

99 Ansari, Fahad and Uzma Karim, *Hijab & Democracy: The Ways of, and Against Secular Fundamentalism*, Islamic Human Rights Commission, United Kingdom, November 2004.

100 "Annual Report", Islamic Human Rights Commission, United Kingdom, 2008, http://www.ihrc.org.uk/show.php?id=3717

101 Feheem, Minutes of Meeting, July 12, 2008, http://www.museire.com/PDF/MINUTES_July_12th_and_June_14th.pdf

102 Metropolitan France is used to refer to the territory in mainland Europe that excludes Corsica and all its colonial territories.

103 "Éléments d'analyse géographique de l'implantation des religions en France", IFOP, December 2006, http://www.ifop.com/europe/docs/religions_geo.pdf

104 Also known as *l'affaire du voile islamique* (the 'Islamic veil affair'), and *l'affaire du foulard* (the 'scarf affair').

105 "Islamic Veil Controversy in France", Wikipedia, http://en.wikipedia.org/wiki/Islamic_veil_controversy_in_France#The_veil_affair

106 "Headscarves in the Headlines", *BBC News*, February 10, 2004, http://news.bbc.co.uk/1/hi/world/europe/3476163.stm

107 Faure, Magali and PhilipGouge, "Headscarf Row Erupts in France", *BBC News*, April 25, 2003, http://news.bbc.co.uk/1/hi/world/europe/2975689.stm

108 Connolly, Kate, "Germans to put Muslims through a loyalty test", *Telegraph*, December 31, 2005, http://www.telegraph.co.uk/news/worldnews/europe/germany/1506712/Germans-to-put-Muslims-through-loyalty-test.html

109 "Discrimination in the name of Neutrality", Human Rights Watch, February 26, 2009, http://www.hrw.org/en/reports/2009/02/25/discrimination-name-neutrality

110 Ansari, Fahad and Uzma Karim, *Hijab & Democracy: The Ways of, and Against Secular Fundamentalism*,Islamic Human Rights Commission, United Kingdom, November 2004, 5.

111 "German Court Upholds Muslim Headscarf Ban in Schools", *Spiegel Online*, March 18, 2008, http://www.spiegel.de/international/gemany

112 Ansari & Karim: 2004, p.6

113 Ansari, Fahad and Uzma Karim, *Hijab & Democracy: The Ways of, and Against Secular Fundamentalism*,Islamic Human Rights Commission, United Kingdom, November 2004, 5

114 BBC News, "German Nuns 'Face Headscarf Ban'", *BBC News*, October 10, 2004, http://news.bbc.co.uk/1/hi/world/europe/3731368.stm

115 Fahad Ansari and Uzma Karim, *Hijab & Democracy: The Ways of, and Against Secular Fundamentalism* (United Kingdom: Islamic Human Rights Commission, November 2004), 5

116 Larsson, Göran, "Muslims in the EU: Sweden", Open Society Institute, EU Monitoring and Advocacy Program,2007, http://www.eumap.org/topics/minority/reports/eumuslims/background_reports/download/sweden/sweden.pdf

117 "Sweden: Government confirms right to headscarf", *Islam in Europe*, January 24, 2007, http://islamineurope.blogspot.com/2007/01/sweden-govt-confirms-right-to-headscarf

118 "Student receives damages for headscarf slight", *The Local*, December 13, 2008, http://www.thelocal.se/

119 For more information, please refer to: http://www.islamonline.net/English/News/2003-09/01/article09.shtml

120 Lamb, Christina, "Headscarf War Threatens to Split Turkey", *Times Online*, May 6, 2007, http://www.timesonline.co.uk/tol/news/world/middle_east/article1752230.ece

121 Knight, India, "Muslims are the new Jews", *Times Online*, October 15, 2006, http://www.timesonline.co.uk/article/0,,24390-2404281.html

122 Walker, Jonathan, "Birmingham a Model for Muslim Women – Report", *Birmingham Post*, January 24, 2008, http://www.birminghampost.net/news/west-midlands-news/tm

Bibliography

Books

Alarcon, Abu Maryam Isma'eel, trans., *Three Essays on the Obligation of Veiling*, Al-Ibaanah Book Publishing, USA, 2003.

Alvi, Sajida Sultana, Homa Hoodfar, and Sheila Mcdonough, *The Muslim Veil in North America: Issues and Debates*, Women's Press, Canada, 2003.

Al-Qarni, A'id, *You Can Be The Happiest Woman In The World: A Treasure Chest of Reminders*, International Islamic Publishing House, Saudi Arabia, 2005.

Allievi, Stefano and Jorgen Nielsen, *Muslim Networks And Transnational Communities In And Across Europe*, Brill USA, Leiden-Boston, 2003.

Bin Abd Alazeez Almusnad, Muhammad, *Adornment of Women, Vision Printing*, Publishing & Distribution, Pakistan, 2002.

Bin Abdullaah bin Baaz, S. Abdul-Azeez, *The Danger of Women Participating in the Work Arena of Men*, Message of Islam, United Kingdom, 1997.

Bin Abdullaah bin Baaz, S. Abdul-Azeez, Muhammad Bin Saalih Al-Uthaimeen, and Zayd Bin Haadee Al-Madkhalee, *The Obligation of Veiling*, Al-Ibaanah Book Publishing, USA, 2003.

Bin Abd Alazeez Almusnad, *Adornment of Women in Forensic and Medical Perspective*, Vision Printing, Publishing & Distribution, Pakistan, 2002.

Hunter, Shireen T., *Islam, Europe's Second Religion: The New Social, Cultural, and Political Landscape*, The Center for Strategic and International Studies, USA, 2002.

Ibn Baz, Shaykh and Shaykh Uthaymeen, *Muslim Minorities – Fatawa Regarding Muslims Living as Minorities*, Message of Islam, United Kingdom, 1998.

Ibrahim, Yasmin, *I Can Wear My Hijab Anywhere!* The Islamic Foundation, United Kingdom, 2004.

Joly, Daniele, *Britannia's Crescent:Making a Place for Muslims in British Society*, Ashgate Publishing Ltd, United Kingdom, 1995.

Lindley, J., A. Dale and S. Dex,, *Ethnic Differences in Women's Demographic, Family Characteristics and Economic Activity Profiles, 1992-2002*, Labour Market Trends, April 2004.

Mernissi, Fatima, *Beyond the Veil*, Saqi Books, United Kingdom, 2003.

Nazlee, Shazia, *The Hijab: Dress for Every Muslimah – An Encouragement and Clarification*, Jam'iat 'Ihyaa' Minhaaj al-Sunnah, United Kingdom, 2005.

Obaidullah Almuslim, Muhammad, trans., *Adornment of Women in Forensic and Medical Perspective*, Vision Printing, Publishing & Distribution, Pakistan, 2002.

Sahgal, Gita and Nire Yuval-Davis, *Refusing Holy Orders: Women and Fundamentalism in Britain*, Women Living Under Muslim Laws, United Kingdom, 2000.

Women Living Under Muslim Laws, *Plan of Action – Dhaka 1997*, WLUML, United Kingdom, 1999. Also available at:
http://www.wluml.org/node/451

Technical Reports

Ansari, Fahad and Uzma Karim, "Hijab & Democracy: The Ways of, and Against Secular Fundamentalism", Islamic Human Rights Commission, United Kingdom, November 2004.

Ameli, Saied R. and Arzu Merali, "Hijab, Meaning, Identity, Otherization and Politics: British Muslim Women", Islamic Human Rights Commission, United Kingdom, January 2006.

Botcherby, S., "Moving On Up? Ethnic Minority Women at Work", Equal Opportunities Commission, United Kingdom, September 2006.

Department for Communities and Local Government, "Engaging with Muslim Women: A Report from the Prime Minister's Event (10 May 2006)", Communities and Local Government Publications, September 2006, http://www.womenandequalityunit.gov.uk/publications/muslimwomenfeedrep.pdf

Department for Communities and Local Government, "Preventing Violent Extremism: Winning Hearts and Minds", Communities and Local Government Publications, United Kingdom, April 2007.

Department for Communities and Local Government, "Empowering Muslim Women: Case Studies", Communities and Local Government Publications, United Kingdom, January 2008.

DfES, "Religious Education in Faith Schools", April 27, 2006, http://findoutmore.dfes.gov.uk/2006/02/religious_educa.html

Dobs, Joy, Hazel Green and Linda Zealey, eds., "Focus on Ethnicity and Religion", National Statistics, 2006, 66, http://www.statistics.gov.uk/downloads/theme_compendia/foer2006/FoER_Main.pdf

Fawcett Society, "The Veil, Feminism and Muslim Women, Fawcett Society", United Kingdom, December 2006, http://www.fawcettsociety.org.uk/documents/Veil%20debate%20report.pdf

Human Rights Watch, "Discrimination in the Name of Neutrality: Headscarf Bans for Teachers and Civil Servants in Germany", United States of America, February 2009, http://www.hrw.org/en/reports/2009/02/25/discrimination-name-neutrality-0

International Crisis Group, "Islam and Identity in Germany", Europe Report No 181, United Kingdom, March 2007.

Islamic Human Rights Commission, "British Anti-Terrorism Policy and the MEK", United Kingdom, May 2006.

Islamic Human Rights Commission, "Muslim Women, Human Rights and Religious Freedom: Europe under the Spotlight of National and International Law", United Kingdom, March 2004.

Larsson, Göran, "Muslims in the EU: Cities Report Sweden", Open Society Institute EU Monitoring and Advocacy Program, 2007, http://www.eumap.org/topics/minority/reports/eumuslims/background_reports/download/sweden/sweden.pdf

Muslim Council of Britain, "Muslims in the Workplace: A Good Practice Guide for Employers and Employees", United Kingdom, March 2005.

Muslim Council of Britain, "Religious Discrimination at Work", United Kingdom, http://www.mcb.org.uk/faith/A5leaflet.pdf

Office for National Statistics, "Religion In The UK". In Census 2001, United Kingdom, February 13, 2003, http://www.statistics.gov.uk/cci/nugget.asp?id=293

Papers, Articles & Periodicals

Ahmed, S., "Women Slipping Thru' The Gaps", *Q-News*, March 13, 2005, pp.3.

Nielsen, Jorgen S., "Islam, Muslims, And British Local And Central Government". Centre for the Study of Islam and Christian – Muslim Relations, United Kingdom, May 1992.

Abrar, Volume 3, No. 5 (53), September 1-15, 2006, Abrar Islamic Foundation, United Kingdom.

Islam21, Issue No. 40, January 2006, International Forum for Islamic Dialogue, United Kingdom.

Return Review, Volume 10, Issue 7, July 2006, The Publishing Return Centre, United Kingdom.

The Muslim Community In Ireland: Challenging Some Of Myths & Misinformation, August 2006, National Consultative Committee on Racism and Interculturalism, Ireland.

Online Articles & Papers

Asaad Buaras, Elham, "Blair Gets Easy Ride from Muslim Women", the *Muslim News,* May 2006, http://www.muslimnews.co.uk/paper/index.php?article=2437

Akhtar, Zeeshan, "Muslim Women Look to the Future", the *Muslim News,* April 2006, http://www.muslimnews.co.uk/paper/index.php?article=2420

Alam, Fareena, "My Battle is in the Living Room", *The Guardian,* March 30, 2003, http://observer.guardian.co.uk/islam/story/0,,925719,00.html

Alam, Fareena, "We must move beyond the hijab", *The Guardian,* November 29, 2005, http://www.guardian.co.uk/education/2005/nov/29/highereducation.uk

Al Yafai, Faisal, "Livingstone Attacks French Headscarf Ban", *The Guardian,* July 13, 2004, http://www.guardian.co.uk/uk/2004/jul/13/schools.schoolsworldwide

Bee, Peta, "Running Under Cover", *The Guardian,* November 20, 2007, http://www.guardian.co.uk/uk/2007/nov/20/race.healthandwellbeing

Beckfordm, Martin, "Baroness Warsi: Labour's Young Muslim Advisory Group is Patronising and Divisive", *Telegraph,* October 7, 2008, http://www.telegraph.co.uk/news/newstopics/politics/labour/3155177/Baroness-Warsi-Labours-Young-Muslim-Advisory-Group-is-patronising-and-divisive.html

Browne, Anthony, "Islamic Fascism", *Daniel Pipes,* February 4, 2006, http://www.danielpipes.org/comments/33783

Boulange, Antoine, "The Hijab, Racism and the State", *International Socialism,* spring 2004, http://pubs.socialistreviewindex.org.uk/isj102/boulange.htm

Cambrensis, Giraldus, "Muslim Burkas Damage Babies' Health", *Western Resistance,* July 31, 2006, http://www.westernresistance.com/blog/archives/002688.html

Casciani, Dominic and Cindi John, "Muslim Modesty in the Spotlight", *BBC News,* March 3, 2005, http://news.bbc.co.uk/go/pr/fr/-/1/hi/uk/4315839.stm

Clement, Joan and Evans-Pritchard Ambrose, "Crackdown on Radicals as Dutch Mourn Film Maker", *Telegraph,* November 10, 2004, http://www.telegraph.co.uk/news/main.jhtml?xml=/news/2004/11/10/wneth10.xml&sSheet=/portal/2004/11/10/ixportal.html

"College's Headscarf Ban Prompts Complaint", *United Press International,* February 12, 2009, http://www.upi.com/Top_News/2009/02/12/Colleges-headscarf-ban-prompts-complaint/UPI-42891234456821/

Dear, Paula, "Women Vow to Protect Muslim Hijab", *BBC News,* June 14, 2004, http://news.bbc.co.uk/1/hi/uk/3805733.stm

Erdem, Suna, "Judges Defy Government To Uphold Turkey Headscarf Ban", *Times Online,* June 6, 2008, http://www.timesonline.co.uk/tol/news/world/europe/article4076180.ece

Faure, Magali and Philip Gouge, "Headscarf Row Erupts in France", *BBC News*, April 25, 2003, http://news.bbc.co.uk/1/hi/world/europe/2975689.stm

Furlong, Ray, "German 'Muslim test' stirs anger", *BBC News*, February 2006, http://news.bbc.co.uk/1/hi/world/europe/4655240.stm

Gerard, Jasper, "Jasper Gerard meets Shabina Begum: Faith, the veil, shopping and me", *Times Online*, March 26, 2006, http://www.timesonline.co.uk/tol/news/article696181.ece?token=null&offset=0&page=1

"German Court Upholds Muslim Headscarf Ban in Schools", *Spiegel Online*, March 18, 2008, http://www.spiegel.de/international/germany/0,1518,542211,00.html

"German Nuns 'Face Headscarf Ban'", *BBC News*, October 10, 2004, http://news.bbc.co.uk/1/hi/world/europe/3731368.stm

Glynn, Sarah, "Liberalising Islam: Creating Brits of the Islamic Persuasion", The University of Edinburgh, April 2008, http://www.geos.ed.ac.uk/homes/sglynn/Liberalising_Islam.pdf

Gupta, Rahila, "An all-too familiar affair", *The Guardian*, February 21, 2009, http://www.guardian.co.uk/commentisfree/belief/2009/feb/20/rushdie-fatwa-religion

Hall, Macer, "At Last The Veil Banned in Class", *Daily Express*, May 7, 2007, http://www.express.co.uk/posts/view/6377

Harding, Jeremy, "What to Wear to School", *London Review of Books*, February 19, 2004, http://www.lrb.co.uk/v26/n04/hard01_.html

"Headscarves in the Headlines", *BBC News*, February 10, 2004, http://news.bbc.co.uk/1/hi/world/europe/3476163.stm

Helm, Toby, "Back British values or lose grants, Kelly tells Muslim groups," *Telegraph*, October 12, 2006, http://www.telegraph.co.uk/news/uknews/1531226/Back-British-values-or-lose-grants,-Kelly-tells-Muslim-groups.html

"Islamic Veil Controversy in France", *Wikipedia*, http://en.wikipedia.org/wiki/Islamic_veil_controversy_in_France/

"Islamic Games Give British Women the Option", the *Muslim News*, September 9, 2005, http://www.themuslimnews.co.uk/news/news.php?article=9902

John, Cindi, "Police Hope for Muslim head Start", *BBC News*, April 24, 2001, http://news.bbc.co.uk/1/hi/uk/1294417.stm

Johnson, B., "The Shabina Begum Case Never Had Anything to do With Modesty", *Telegraph*, March 23, 2006, http://www.telegraph.co.uk/opinion/main.jhtml?xml=/opinion/2006/03/23/do2303.xml&sSheet=/news/2006/03/23/ixnewstop.html

Johnston, Philip, "Muslims To Pay School's Legal Fight To Uphold Niqab Ban", *Telegraph*, April 19, 2008, http://www.telegraph.co.uk/news/uknews/1541632/Muslims-to-pay-schools-legal-fight-to-uphold-niqab-ban.html

Khan, Amil, "*Ninjabies* Learn To Fight Back In Britain", *Reuters*, May 3, 2007, http://uk.reuters.com/article/idUKL0250204920070503?sp=true

Knight, India, "Muslims are the new Jews", *Times Online*, October 15, 2006, http://www.timesonline.co.uk/article/0,,24390-2404281.html

"Horrific Attack by Train Staff on Young Girl for Wearing Hijab", *MPAUK*, June 12, 2006, http://www.mpacuk.org/content/view/2222/1/

"IHRC on CNN: Singapore, Hijab Ban, Muslim and Minority Rights", *Islamic Human Rights Commission*, August 11, 2006, http://www.ihrc.org.uk/show.php?id=760

"Islam and Muslims in Europe", *Euro-Islam.Info*, October 25, 2005,
http://www.euro-islam.info/pages/news_germany_archive_10-05.html

"Islam, Children's Rights, and the Hijab-gate of Rah-e-Kargar", *Worker-Communist Party of Iran*, June 1997,
http://www.m-hekmat.com/en/1035en.html

"Lord Chief Justice: Sharia can be a 'basis for mediation' in the UK", *Islam Today*, July 5, 2008,
http://www.islamtoday.com/showme2.cfm?cat_id=38&sub_cat_id=1933

Malik, K., "Born in Bradford", *Prospect*, October 2005,
http://www.kenanmalik.com/essays/bradford_prospect.html

"Meco Supports Niqab Ban in Schools", *MECO*, February 1, 2007,
http://www.meco.org.uk/press18.htm

Mendick, Robert and Kiran Randhawa, "Muslim Girl's Brother Linked to Islam Radicals", *London Evening Standard*, March 4, 2005,
http://www.thisislondon.co.uk/news/article17038092details/Muslim+girl%27s+brother+linked+to+Islam+radicals/article.do

"Minister, Mayor Backs British Muslim Football Team", the *Muslim News*, September 16, 2005,
http://www.muslimnews.co.uk/index/press.php?pr=214

Moniquet, Claude, "The Radicalisation of Muslim Youth in Europe: The Real Scale of the Threat", *Agentura*, April 2005,
http://www.agentura.ru/english/experts/euroislaism

"Muslim Girls Urged to Join Police", *BBC News*, March 16, 2005,
http://news.bbc.co.uk/go/pr/fr/-/1/hi/england/lancashire/4353475.stm

"Muslim Groups Patronising", *Asian Image*, October 27, 2008,
http://www.asianimage.co.uk/uk/3796060.Muslim_groups__patronising_/

"Muslim Women Get Ahead in MET", *BBC News*, April 25, 2001,
http://news.bbc.co.uk/1/hi/world/europe/1297286.stm

"Muslim Women Offered Job Support", *BBC News*, February 25, 2006,
http://news.bbc.co.uk/1/hi/england/leicestershire/4750612.stm

"Muslim women to advise Government on preventing violent extremism", Communities and Local Government Department website, November 21, 2007,
http://www.communities.gov.uk/news/corporate/554064

"Muslims in Europe: Country Guide", *BBC News*, December 23, 2005,
http://news.bbc.co.uk/1/hi/world/europe/4385768.stm

Namazie, Maryam, "Political Islam is the Problem", *Worker-Communist Party of Iran*, July 18, 2005,
http://www.wpiran.org/English/wb185%20Political%20Islam%20is%20the%20Problem%20on%2077%20london%20attack%20mn.htm

Norfolk, Andrew, "Muslim Group Behind 'Mega-Mosque' Seeks To Convert All Britain", *Times Online*, September 10, 2007,
http://www.timesonline.co.uk/tol/comment/faith/article2419524.ece

Norfolk, Andrew, "Dewsbury: Kidnap, Lynching And A Suicide", *Times Online*, May 28, 2008,
http://www.timesonline.co.uk/tol/news/uk/crime/article4016574.ece

Panorama, "Muslims Facing Most Faith Bias", *BBC News*, November 22, 2004,
http://news.bbc.co.uk/1/hi/programmes/panorama/4171456.stm

Press Association, "Veil Row Teacher Sacked", *The Guardian*, November 24, 2006,
http://www.guardian.co.uk/education/2006/nov/24/schools.uk

Robinson, Nina, "Muslims 'face barriers' Over Sport", *BBC News*, August 25, 2006,
http://news.bbc.co.uk/go/pr/fr/-/1/hi/uk/5286568.stm

Rozenberg, Joshua, "Muslim Girl, 12, Loses Court Battle For Right To Wear Veil In Lessons", *Telegraph*, February 22, 2007,
http://www.telegraph.co.uk/news/uknews/1543476/Muslim-girl-12-loses-court-battle-for-right-to-wear-veil-in-lessons.html

Sands, Sarah, "The Very Unorthodox Views Of Cameron's First Muslim Shadow Minister", *Daily Mail*, July 9, 2007,
http://www.dailymail.co.uk/femail/article-467103/The-unorthodox-views-Camerons-Muslim-Shadow-Minister.html

"School wins Muslim Dress Appeal", *BBC News*, March 22, 2006,
http://news.bbc.co.uk/go/pr/fr/-/1/hi/education/4832072.stm

"Schoolgirl Wins Muslim Gown Case", *BBC News*, March 2, 2005,
http://news.bbc.co.uk/1/hi/england/beds/bucks/herts/4310545.stm

"Siddiqui welcomes High Court judgment on Jilbab controversy", *The Muslim Parliament of Great Britain*, June 15, 2004,
http://www.muslimparliament.org.uk/Jilbab.htm

Simpson, Peter Vinthagen, "Student Receives Damages For Headscarf Slight", *The Local*, December 13, 2008,
http://www.thelocal.se/16328/20081213/

Smith, Laura, "My Manager Said I Looked Like a Terrorist", *The Guardian*, September 7, 2006,
http://www.guardian.co.uk/print/0,,329570618-103680,00.html

Special Correspondent, "Higher Education Institutions Obstacles to Muslim Women", the *Muslim News*, August 25, 2006, 10,
http://higher-education-news.newslib.com/story/217-3242437/

"Speed Dating – Muslim Style", *BBC News*, August 19, 2003,
http://news.bbc.co.uk/go/pr/fr/-/1/hi/wales/south_east/3164067.stm

Straw, Jack, "I felt uneasy talking to someone I couldn't see", *The Guardian*, October 6, 2006,
http://politics.guardian.co.uk/labour/story/0,,1888847,00.html#article_continue.

"Survey finds support for veil ban", *BBC News*, November 29, 2006,
http://news.bbc.co.uk/1/hi/uk/6194032.stm

"Sweden: Gov't Confirms Right To Headscarf", *Islam in Europe*, January 24, 2007,
http://islamineurope.blogspot.com/2007/01/sweden-govt-confirms-right-to-headscarf.html

Tavernise, Sabrina, "Turkey Moves To Lift Head Scarf Ban At Universities", *International Herald Tribune*, February 10, 2008,
http://www.iht.com/articles/2008/02/10/europe/turkey.php

Taylor, Matthew, "Two-Thirds Oppose State Aided Faith Schools", *The Guardian*, August 23, 2005,
http://education.guardian.co.uk/faithschools/story/0,13882,1554593,00.html

"Thinly Veiled", *The Friday Thing*, August 11, 2006,
http://www.thefridayproject.co.uk/hi/tft/culture_and_society/002139.php

Triggle, Nick, "Dress Code Deters Muslim Medics", *BBC News*, June 29, 2006,
http://news.bbc.co.uk/go/pr/fr/-/1/hi/health/4634351.stm

"Veil harms equal right – Harman," *BBC News*, October 11, 2006,
http://news.bbc.co.uk/1/hi/uk_politics/6040016.stm

Versi, Ahmed J, "Giving Muslims a Voice", *Muslim Council of Britain*, August 18, 2004,
http://www.mcb.org.uk/features/features.php?ann_id=442

Wajid, Sara, "Enter the Ninjabi: More Muslim Women Take up Martial Arts in Britain", *Gulf Times*, June 21, 2007,
http://www.gulf-times.com/mritems/streams/2007/6/20/2_156296_1_255.pdf

Wajid, Sara, "The Ninjabies – Muslim Women In The Modern City", *Intercultural Cities Conference,* May 1, 2008, http://interculturalcities.wordpress.com/2008/05/01/the-ninjabis-muslim-women-in-the-modern-city/

Walker, Jonathan, "Birmingham a Model for Muslim Women – Report", *Birmingham Post,* January 24, 2008, http://www.birminghampost.net/news/west-midlands-news/tm

Weeke, Stephen, "Italian Woman Ticketed for Wearing a Burqa", *NBC News,* September 21, 2004, http://www.prohijab.net/english/italy-hijab-news.htm

"What Are The Issues Related To The Headscarf Ban In France?", *Association for Women's Rights in Development,* February 12, 2008, http://www.awid.org/eng/Issues-and-Analysis/Library/What-are-the-issues-related-to-the-headscarf-ban-in-France

"Will Dropping the Hijab make Women Safer?", *Times Online,* August 4, 2005, http://www.timesonline.co.uk/article/0,,564-1720876,00.html

"Women Hit back over Hijab Ruling", *BBC News,* September 8, 2005, http://news.bbc.co.uk/go/pr/fr/-/1/hi/uk/4742869.stm

Websites

Al-Huda, http://www.alhudapk.com//home/about-us

Association of Muslim Schools Statistics, http://www.amsuk.org/index.php?option=com_content&task=view&id=13&Itemid=45

The City Circle, http://www.thecitycircle.com/

Islamic Circles, Muslim Marriage Events, http://www.muslimmarriageevents.org/

MPACUK, http://www.mpacuk.org/content/view/2046/98/

MPUK, http://www.muslimprofessionals.org.uk

Musawah, http://www.musawah.org

TV Programmes and Documentary

"Futuristic Islam", Shariah TV, by Tazeen Ahmed, *Channel 4,* August 10, 2006.

"Growing Up Muslim in Britain", Shariah TV, by Tazeen Ahmed, *Channel 4,* London, August 8, 2006.

"Hijab Trials", City Sisters, *Islam Channel,* http://www.islamchannel.tv/citysisters/HijabTrial.aspx

"Me and the Mosque", by Zarqa Nawas, National Film Board of Canada, 2005, 52 min 45 s, http://www.onf-nfb.gc.ca/fra/collection/film/?id=51517

"Sex and Relationships", Shariah TV, by Tazeen Ahmed, *Channel 4,* London, August 9, 2006.

"What Muslims Want", Dispatches, *Channel 4,* London, August 8, 2006.

"Women Only Jihad", Dispatches, by Tazeen Ahmed, *Channel 4,* London, October 30, 2006, http://video.google.co.uk/videoplay?docid=-3046570183637153703&q=dispatches

"Women's Dress", Shariah TV, *Channel 4,* London, http://channel4.com/culture/microsites/S/shariahtv2/expression3.html

About the author

Ayesha Salma Kariapper was born in Lahore, Pakistan. She was educated at the Lahore University of Management Sciences in Pakistan and the Institute of Social Studies at The Hague in The Netherlands. She has lived in London since 2005, working as an independent researcher and a development professional. She has held varied roles in both the human rights and international development sectors in the United Kingdom and Pakistan. She has several years' experience of managing development projects in South Asia and Africa particularly in maternal and child health, formal and non-formal education and rights awareness among women and girls. Her research interests include social movements, peasant struggles and women's rights.

Index

A

Afghanistan *ix, xiv, 4, 22, 75*
Al-Huda *6, 74, 105*
An-Nisa Women's Society *29*

B

British Muslim:
    community *1, 4, 17, 19, 25-26, 30, 53, 56, 58, 60, 63, 65, 67, 70, 75, 85, 94*
    identity *44, 48*
    women *1, 2, 4-5, 20, 24, 27-29, 43, 67, 70, 75-76, 80, 82, 101-104*
burqa (or burka) *ix, 38, 40, 85, 93, 95-96, 105*

C

chador *ix*
community activism *20, 30, 94, 99*

D

dars (or dars-e-Qur'an) *ix, 10, 30*
discrimination:
    gender *2, 28-29, 54-54, 64, 68, 73, 91, 102*
    racial *3, 19, 68*
    religious *64-65, 68, 71, 83-84, 102*
    religious freedom *57-58, 91, 93-94, 96*
dress *xii, 2-3, 5-7, 9, 12, 15, 22, 27, 31, 34-38, 40, 50, 58-60, 63, 67-68, 70-71, 73, 77, 93, 95, 97, 99*
dress codes ideology *30, 34, 37-38, 45, 47, 50, 52, 58*
    the politics of *1, 13, 29, 36, 58, 63, 72, 76, 79, 83-84, 92, 98, 102*
dupatta *ix, xii, 37, 40, 42*

E

empowerment *4, 34, 55*
    strategies *55*
    women's *4, 103*
Europe *7, 57, 83, 87, 93, 106*
European Convention on Human Rights *83*

F

face-veil *1, 64-66*
    full-face veil *xi, 1, 62-63, 89, 95, 101, 105*
    see also niqab
feminism *3, 13, 27, 67, 82, 88-89, 92, 98, 101, 103*
fiqh *xii*
France *44, 83, 86 90, 92, 94, 110*
fundamentalism *5, 21, 46-47, 62, 67, 73, 83, 101-102*

G

gender *5, 6, 22, 38, 45, 52, 54, 61, 72, 94*
    equality *4, 37, 83*
    roles *1, 27-28, 32, 44, 48-49, 51-53, 56, 65, 70, 79, 101*
Germany *44, 83, 90-91, 94*

H

hadith *ix, xiv, 27*
hajj *ix, 40*
halal *x, 19-20, 43, 48*
haram *x*
Hizb ut-Tahrir *61-62*

I

identity: assertion *19*
    Muslim *22, 26, 37, 44, 48, 94*
    religious *22, 26, 28, 48, 88*
integration *7, 19, 26, 44, 46, 48, 52, 54, 86, 94, 98*
International Women's Islamic Games *75-76, 78*
Ireland *15, 83-85*
Islamic Human Rights Commission *83, 110*
Islamist *xiv, 60-62, 66, 67*
Islamophobia *40, 54, 99*

J

jilbab *x, 2, 7, 27, 31, 36, 38, 56-57, 60-61, 65*

K

kalimah *x, 6*

khimar *x, 39*

L

labour market *17, 69, 95*

laïcité *86, 88-89*

M

mahram *x, xi, 33, 34, 81*

multiculturalism *4, 19-22, 24-26, 44, 54, 59, 73, 86, 94, 96, 98, 103-104*

Muslim Council of Britain (MCB) *see sports*

Muslim Public Affairs Committee UK *27-29*

Muslim Women's Sports Foundation (MWSF) *76, 80*

N

National Muslim Women's Advocacy Group (NMWAG) *23*

niqab *x-xi, 1, 3, 27, 30-31, 36, 62-67, 81, 83, 85-86, 89, 93, 101, 105*

P

Pakistan *ix, xii-xiv, 3, 7, 9, 15-16, 36, 86, 94*

patriarchy *3, 5, 20, 44, 55, 67, 101*

Q

Qur'an *ix, xi-xiii, 6, 39, 66, 83*

R

Race Relations Act *63, 71*

racial discrimination: *see discrimination*

racism *1-2, 10, 19-21, 47, 54, 57, 68, 99, 101-102*

       anti-racism *7, 20-21, 103*

religious: *see discrimination, school, identity*

S

Saudi Arabia *x-xi, xiii-xiv, 4, 35-36*

school:

       religious *5, 20, 45-49, 50-51, 53-54, 108*

       secularism in schools *49, 86-87*

secularism *3, 13, 21-22, 24, 27, 45, 48, 67, 82, 86-89, 97, 98, 103*

sexual discrimination: *see discrimination*
shalwar kameez *ix, xii, 9, 36-37, 40, 56, 58-60, 69*
Shari'a *x, xii*
social cohesion *7, 19, 24-26, 46, 52, 103*
Southall Black Sisters *21*
sports:
    Muslim Council of Britain (MCB) *11, 19, 26, 37, 57, 65*
    participation *12, 51, 74-77, 79, 80-81*
Sunnah *xii*
Sunni *xii-xiii, 83*
surah *x, xiii, 6*
Sweden *83, 94-95*

T
Tablighi Jama'at *xiii, 6, 65, 67, 105*
tafseer *xiii, 10, 30, 40, 42, 74*
terrorist attacks *22-23, 25, 65, 85, 106-107*
Turkey *xii, 12, 82-83, 86, 94, 97-98, 110*

U
Ummah *xiii, 37*
United Kingdom (UK) *xiii, 1, 4, 7, 15, 20, 35, 55, 61, 80, 83, 98*

V
veiling *ix-x, 3, 6-7, 13, 27, 31, 34-39, 55, 66, 73, 95, 99, 102, 107*
    veiling practices *3, 5, 8, 72, 98,*
    see also dress

W
Wahhabism *xiii-xiv, 35, 38, 66*
Women Against Fundamentalisms (WAF) *21*